CONFIDENT
FAITH

BUILDING A FIRM F[...]BELIEFS

FOREWORD BY LEE STROBEL

MARK MITTELBERG

 TYNDALE HOUSE PUBLISHERS, INC. • CAROL STREAM, ILLINOIS

Visit Tyndale online at www.tyndale.com.

Visit Mark Mittelberg's website at MarkMittelberg.com.

TYNDALE and Tyndale's quill logo are registered trademarks of Tyndale House
Publishers, Inc.

Confident Faith: Building a Firm Foundation for Your Beliefs

Designed by Erik M. Peterson

Edited by Jane Vogel

Published in association with the literary agency of Alive Communications, Inc.,
7680 Goddard Street, Suite 200, Colorado Springs, CO 80920.

Library of Congress Cataloging-in-Publication Data

Mittelberg, Mark.
   Confident faith : building a firm foundation for your beliefs / Mark Mittelberg.
     pages cm
   Includes bibliographical references.
   ISBN 978-1-4143-2996-3 (pbk.)
  1. Faith. 2. Self-actualization (Psychology)—Religious aspects—Christianity.
  3. Success—Religious aspects—Christianity. 4. Christian life. I. Title.
   BV4637.M55 2013
   230—dc23   2012046188

Printed in the United States of America

19 18 17 16 15 14 13
7   6   5   4   3   2   1

To my wonderful parents, Orland and Virginia Mittelberg,
who patiently and lovingly nudged me toward a confident faith

CONTENTS

TWENTY ARROWS OF TRUTH

TEN BARRIERS TO BELIEF

FOREWORD

by Lee Strobel, author of
The Case for Christ and *The Case for Faith*

I wish this book had been available on January 20, 1980.

That's the day I decided to reevaluate my atheism and consider whether there was any convincing evidence to believe in God—*any* God, whether the God of Islam, Christianity, Mormonism, Judaism, or even the multiplicity of gods in Hinduism. Impressed by my wife's transformation since she had become a Christian, I vowed to use my training in journalism and law (I was the legal-affairs editor of the *Chicago Tribune*) to launch a full-fledged investigation of spiritual matters.

My quest would have been considerably easier if I'd had this invaluable guide at the time. As Mark Mittelberg so brilliantly describes, all of us approach faith in differing ways. Whether we realize it or not, we're influenced by a myriad of factors, some of which can take us toward the truth, while others simply lead us into confusion. These insights would have been extremely helpful as I tried to sort through the competing spiritual beliefs on my own.

You're fortunate—whether you are a committed Christian or someone who is just beginning your own journey of spiritual discovery—that you've now got this terrific guide-book to help you maneuver through the minefield of conflicting and contradictory claims about what is true. Rest assured that you'll find Mark to be a thoughtful, empathetic, and discerning friend—and one who also injects regular doses of humor into the discussion—as you go through this eye-opening and heart-expanding process toward a confident faith.

More than that, Mark will give you *reasons* for such confidence. With unusual clarity, he will walk you through such diverse areas as science, philosophy, history, archaeology, religious experience, and evidence related to the Bible as he presents his "twenty arrows" that point compellingly toward the truth of Christianity.

I can't think of anyone who is better positioned than Mark to serve as your spiritual coach. Yes, he has excellent academic credentials, having earned a graduate degree in philosophy of religion and having been mentored by some of the brightest minds in Christendom. But beyond that, Mark has spent the last few decades helping everyday people find a firm foundation for their beliefs. He lives in the trenches of real life, not in some isolated ivory tower.

His style in this book is to walk alongside you as you weigh competing truth claims and come to your own conclusions about where the evidence convincingly points.

Having been Mark's friend and ministry partner for twenty-five years, I can attest to his sterling character, his godly lifestyle, and his heartfelt desire to assist others as they seek assurance about spiritual truth. His approach is to naturally befriend you as you embark on the most exciting and stimulating journey of your life, helping you affirm for yourself where the truth really resides.

Almost every Monday, Mark and I get together for lunch. It's a routine we started when we worked together in Chicago, continued when we lived in Southern California, and carry on now in Colorado, where both of our families now reside. It's one of the highlights of my week because I'm constantly learning something new from him. We talk about the mundane and the lofty, but we frequently circle back to discussing how we can know for sure that our spiritual beliefs are well placed. One thing amazes me: Mark's deep reservoir of wisdom never runs dry.

So please pull up a chair and join us. Wherever you are in your spiritual adventure, you're going to find yourself encouraged and challenged. But most of all, you're going to walk away with everything you need to find a truly confident faith in Jesus Christ.

HOW TO USE THIS BOOK

We all believe things we hope are true. But how can we be sure? How can we be confident we've made the right faith commitments and that our beliefs are built on a solid foundation of facts?

For example, if you're a Christian, how certain are you that your faith is based on reliable information—that it's really true? This book will help you answer that question. And if you believe something other than Christianity, how can you test your beliefs to see if they square with reality? We'll address that issue, as well.

Here's an overview of the sections of this book and how they are designed to serve you:

- First, there's an introductory chapter that will examine the meaning of *faith* and explore who has faith and how it affects them. (*Spoiler Alert:* everyone is affected!) Then, in the first chapter of the section called "Six Faith Paths," there is a simple, fun-to-take questionnaire that will help you discover your current approach to faith—how you arrived at the beliefs you're now trusting in.

- Next, over the remaining chapters in that section we'll unpack each of the faith paths, one per chapter. This will help you not only better understand (and perhaps reinforce) the approach you've been using to determine your beliefs but also to gain wisdom about the pros and cons of each of the six approaches. This can serve to show you how to better ground your beliefs on a foundation of truth, and it can help you better understand how your friends and family members got to where they are in their beliefs. There is also a chapter at the end of the section that will help you compare and weigh the six approaches we've discussed.

- After that, we'll apply what we've learned, especially as it relates to the sixth faith path, by exploring "Twenty Arrows of Truth" that point to the truth of the Christian faith. These will be presented over three chapters, the first of which deals with arguments from science and logic, the second with evidence related to and supportive of the Bible, and the third with information gained from history as well as human experience. The cumulative impact of this information will be to strengthen your confidence in the truth of Christianity. (Or, if you're not a Christian, it will help you understand the logic and evidence that supports it and give you a wealth of data to study and consider.) Also, the "Twenty Arrows" section will serve as a ready reference tool in the future, as you get into conversations about matters of faith and want to look back at these succinctly summarized arguments.

- Finally, the closing section, called "Ten Barriers to Belief," will identify some of the common impediments that hold us back in the journey toward confident faith. This might help you discover roadblocks you'll need to overcome in your own life, and it could also aid you in understanding and encouraging others who lack confidence in what they believe. This section ends with a short account of how the author first found *faith* . . . and then *confidence* in that faith. More than that, it presents a vision for how your own confident faith can impact the world.

CHAPTER ONE

WHAT IS FAITH AND WHO HAS IT?

Faith is the confidence that what we hope for will actually happen; it gives us assurance about things we cannot see.

HEBREWS 11:1

Think about your day so far.

This morning, you got up and had something to eat—*by faith*—trusting that nobody had laced your food with poison. Perhaps you stopped by a coffee shop and you relied on the character behind the counter not to put some kind of harmful substance in your triple-shot, extra-foam latte. You got to work—maybe even took an elevator?—and sat in an office chair without testing it first to see if it was strong enough to hold you. (This can be a highly dangerous activity. I read once—and I know it *had* to be true because it was on the Internet—that someone sat on what turned out to be a defective chair; it broke, the man was injured, and the accident led to his eventual death! So you just can't be too careful.)

You started your computer and typed in some confidential information, even though you knew that the latest Internet virus could hijack that information and broadcast it to everyone in your address book. During your lunch break you went out for a walk and paused to pat a stranger's dog, assuming you would not join the ranks of the 4.7 million Americans bitten by a dog each year (of whom, on average, 2,425 require medical attention *every day*).[1]

Then, at the end of the day, you steered your car onto the road and headed home, trusting (but not really knowing) that some sixteen-year-old NASCAR wannabe wouldn't be out drag racing his friends and come careening toward you at an extreme rate of speed.

No doubt about it—you live your life by faith every day, even in the mundane details. What is faith? My broad definition is *beliefs and actions that are based on something considered to be trustworthy—even in the absence of absolute proof.*

You believed the food was safe, so you ate it; you trusted the chair would hold you, so you sat in it; you've had luck in the past with computers, random canines, and commutes home—so why not try them again? You didn't have conclusive evidence that any of these things would work out, but the odds seemed to be in your favor, so you went for it. All of us do similar things—routinely.

We live by faith not only in the small, everyday details of ordinary experience but also in the bigger issues related to religion, God, and eternity. We all adopt "beliefs and actions" related to these areas, "based on something we consider to be trustworthy—even in the absence of absolute proof." So if you are a Christian, you're trusting in the teachings of Christ;

if a Muslim, you're trusting in the teachings of Muhammad; if a Buddhist, you're trusting in the teachings of Buddha.

Even nonreligious people live in the trust that their non-religious beliefs are accurate and that they won't someday face a thoroughly religious Maker who, come to find out, actually did issue a list of guidelines and requirements that they failed to pay attention to.

"Oh, I never worry about things like that," someone may say. But that statement itself is an expression of faith—faith that it's okay not to concern oneself with such matters. You don't know that they are unimportant—you just assume that to be the case. That's part of the person's own particular version of nonreligious faith.

Even well-known atheists like Richard Dawkins and Sam Harris live their lives accepting an unproven assumption that there is no God and that the opinions they express about these matters are ultimately helping and not harming people. They don't *know* they are correct—they just *believe* and *act* as if they are.

In fact, Dawkins, who is probably the best-known activist for atheism of our day, admitted recently that he was only "6.9 out of seven" in terms of his certainty that there is no God, adding, "I think the probability of a supernatural creator existing is very very low."[2] Prior to that, in an interview in *Time* magazine, he acknowledged that "there could be something incredibly grand and incomprehensible and beyond our present understanding."

Biochemist Francis Collins, who was arguing in the interview for the other side, shot back, "That's God."

Dawkins replied, "Yes. But it could be any of a billion

Gods. It could be God of the Martians or of the inhabitants of Alpha Centauri. The chance of its being a particular God, Yahweh, the God of Jesus, is vanishingly small—at the least, the onus is on you to demonstrate why you think that's the case."[3]

Whether the chances are big or small, the important thing to catch here is that Dawkins doesn't know there is no God—he even concedes the possibility that some kind of God might actually exist. Rather, he takes it on *faith* that there actually is no God, and goes on with his routine of belittling people's belief in God and writing books like *The God Delusion*.

Now, I'm sure Dawkins would argue that his is an educated conclusion that is supported by the preponderance of the evidence. But even if he turned out to be right (I'm betting my life he won't), it wouldn't change the fact that his conclusion is a belief that he holds in the absence of real proof. In other words, it's a conclusion that seems to him to be the right one, based on the data he's been willing to examine—but one that goes beyond what can be known with certainty.

That's just the way life is. *We all live by some form of faith—in something.* Which leads us to the central question of this book: Is ours a well-founded faith? A wise faith? A faith that makes sense and is supported by the facts? One that works in real life and is worth hanging on to?

More personally, is yours a faith you've really thought about and intentionally chosen—or did you just slide into it at some point along the way? Is it a faith about which you can be genuinely confident?

→ ←

When I went to college, I came to the painful realization that I'd grown into my faith quite passively. I'd been raised believing in Jesus, trusting in the Bible, and accepting that the church was the carrier of God's truth. I had an unsubstantiated confidence in the truth of all of this.

Then I signed up for a philosophy class. My professor, a religious man with a degree from a radically liberal seminary, seemed to delight in dismantling what he considered to be the simplistic beliefs of many of his Christian students—and I felt like one of his favorite targets. He pointed out problems with the Bible, with what he referred to as "traditional views about God," and with most of the rest of the things I'd been taught. His intellectual onslaught woke me up and made me face the fact that I'd bought into a belief system that I barely understood and had never critically analyzed. My superficial confidence melted away quickly.

Not knowing how to respond, I went to my church for help—but I have to admit that my initial attempts to get answers from some of the leaders there were pretty disheartening. For example, I told one of my adult Sunday school teachers that my faith was being assailed in college and that I needed a deeper understanding not just of what we believed but also of why we thought it was correct.

"How do we know that the Bible is really true," I asked, "and that it is actually God's Word?" I'll never forget his response.

"Oh, that's easy," he replied. "It says right here in the New Testament that 'all scripture is given by inspiration of God, and is profitable for doctrine, for reproof, for correction, for instruction in righteousness.'"[4]

"Yes, I know that verse . . . but how do we know that what it says is true?" I responded.

"Because it says it is," he answered, "and it's the Word of God!"

"But that's the very question we're trying to answer," I shot back. "How do we know it's really the Word of God? If all you do is appeal to the Bible's claims to prove that the Bible is true, then you're guilty of circular reasoning and haven't proved anything."

He gazed at me with a look that betrayed his suspicion that I was rapidly sinking into the quicksand of skepticism—or had already become an actual infidel—and then, with a deep breath, he took another run at me. "You need to realize that there's no higher authority than God's revelation. If God says it's true, then you can bank your life on it."

"Okay," I replied wearily, "but how do you know that God is really the one talking here? Lots of religious books claim to be God talking—like the Qur'an, and the Book of Mormon—but you don't believe those books, do you?"

"Of course not—but that's because," he triumphantly retorted, *those other books are not the Word of God!*"

At this point, I felt like Indiana Jones in that infamous scene in *Raiders of the Lost Ark* where he finally gets fed up with his sword-wielding opponent's antics and pulls out his pistol and shoots the guy. Of course I'm only kidding (at least now I am)—I would never actually shoot anyone! But it was becoming abundantly clear that logic was not going to get me any further in that conversation. So I finally had to let it go—although I was left with the same questions churning in my mind.

Soon thereafter, I'm thankful to say, I found some other teachers and books that proved to be much more helpful. I'll come back to my story later, but this exasperating interchange and other similar ones along the way helped me realize that people hold to all kinds of religious ideas—whether right or wrong—for all kinds of weak and apparently unfounded reasons. I determined then and there that regardless of where I ended up with my faith, my conclusions would be based on more solid criteria than that which some of my teachers were apparently clinging to.

A few years ago I bought a new mountain bike. That may not sound like a big deal to you, but for me it was quite an event. That's because I no longer lived in the Midwest, where most of my "mountain biking" was really more akin to *prairie biking*"—without any mountains or even serious hills. At the time I lived in the foothills of the Santa Ana Mountains of California, and I decided to finally research and invest in a full-suspension, no-nonsense, bona fide mountain bike. So I subscribed to *Mountain Bike Action* magazine, searched for info online, and started reading all kinds of reviews and articles.

I knew I wanted a bike that would be lightweight but also extremely durable. So I studied up on the pros and cons of the various options for frame materials, including steel, aluminum, titanium, and carbon fiber. That last option seemed the most unlikely choice, at least at first, because I was planning on riding some serious trails—with big rocks, sharp turns, and plenty of drops and obstacles—and entrusting my safety to some kind of newfangled synthetic glass or plastic or whatever it was just didn't seem like a good idea.

But I kept reading and researching, doing Google searches, and talking to any expert who would take the time to interact with me. Guess what I learned? Carbon fiber is stronger than aluminum or steel and even lighter than titanium. It's expensive, but it provides a great combination of durability and weight—and it looks awesome, too.

So as you've probably already gathered, I ended up buying a carbon-fiber mountain bike. After months of research, I bought the top frame I could get for the money. I also researched, read reviews, and got expert advice on each of the components to build onto the frame, including the fork, rear shock, crank, derailleurs, shifters, brakes (front and rear hydraulic disc brakes, no less), handlebars, stem, seat post, saddle, wheel sets, tires—I even spent a fair amount of time reading up on the best pedals and riding shoes to purchase.

The result is that I now have a bike I love to ride, and it has served me really well, both when I lived in California and now where I reside in the foothills of the Colorado Rocky Mountains. (Honestly, I think it's about the coolest bike on the planet. It ought to be—I paid the price of a motorcycle but got a cycle without the motor. Worse, *I'm* the motor.)

Why do I explain all this? To point out a sobering fact: many of us spend more time researching, discussing, and seeking wisdom about decisions that are of low to moderate importance—like what bike to purchase, which car or SUV to drive, what clothes to wear, which shrubs or flowers to plant, what university to attend, or (you fill in the blank)—than we do on monumental issues like what we believe about God, how we'll respond to the claims of Jesus and the teachings of the Bible, or where we'll spend eternity. We've got our priorities backward!

Seriously, don't you think it's worth spending some significant time reflecting on your faith? If you're a Christian, I'm optimistic that doing so will enhance and strengthen your beliefs—giving you a more confident faith that will better withstand the challenges of cynical professors, irreligious relatives, and skeptical friends. If you have a different set of beliefs, or no religion at all, then I'm convinced you've got much to gain and little to lose. Regardless of the outcome, energy spent reflecting on these issues will serve to deepen your convictions about what you ultimately put your trust in—and you might discover some exciting truths along the way.

Let me join you. My goal is to help you think through which beliefs about God and your spiritual life are worth hanging on to—that's what we'll discuss in the second section of the book, as we consider what I call "Twenty Arrows of Truth" related to the Christian faith. But before that, in the first section following this introductory chapter, I want to help you consider something most people overlook: *Which approach to deciding what to believe is most helpful?* This is crucial, because the method (or methods) you use in deciding what to believe has a huge bearing on what those beliefs will actually be, as well as how confident you'll feel in holding on to them. So you owe it to yourself not only to think about where you're putting your faith, but also to step back and *think about how you're thinking about it.*[5]

To illustrate the importance of this, let me go back to my mountain bike example. There were a number of ways I could have chosen my bike. I could have simply said, "It's got to be a red one"—and then gone with the first bike that fit that criterion. But it might have turned out to be a horrible red bike. Or I could have said, "It needs to be made in America"—but there are both good bikes and bad bikes made in the USA, so that approach might have led me in a wrong direction as well. Or I could have decided to pick the bicycle I had the best feelings about, regardless of what the reviewers were saying about that particular model. But I've learned long ago that buying things based on "warm fuzzies" is not a good idea. Instead, I decided to do some real research, looking for objective information from qualified experts who would give unbiased opinions—and the result is that I'm confident I made a good choice.

Can you see how the method we use to make these decisions can impact our confidence in what we actually select? What's true about bikes is true about spiritual beliefs as well.

Most people never consider this. They just arbitrarily adopt an approach—or accept one that's been handed to them—and uncritically employ it to choose a set of beliefs that may or may not really add up. So they end up embracing ideas they haven't carefully examined and which they certainly don't feel ready to defend to others (like me in college). I'm sure you don't want to follow their pattern. That's why we're going to unpack six common approaches, or what

I'll be describing as six "faith paths" people take in order to arrive at their spiritual points of view.

The following section will explain those faith paths in practical terms, one per chapter, and help you weigh some of the pros and cons of each one. Before that, though, let me encourage you to fill out the "Faith Path Questionnaire" in the next chapter. Once you've identified which faith path brought you to where you are today, you'll be ready to figure out how that approach impacts your current beliefs (or lack of beliefs), and what steps will help move you toward greater certainty in your faith. More than that, this process can help you better understand your friends and relatives, and equip you to coach them in how they can clarify their own faith commitments.

Let me encourage you to engage fully in this journey. Yes, it will stretch you to think about things you've probably taken for granted, and it might lead you to rethink some beliefs you've long held to. But it also promises to help you build a strong foundation for your beliefs and, in the end, to enjoy the assurance and benefits that come with having a confident faith.

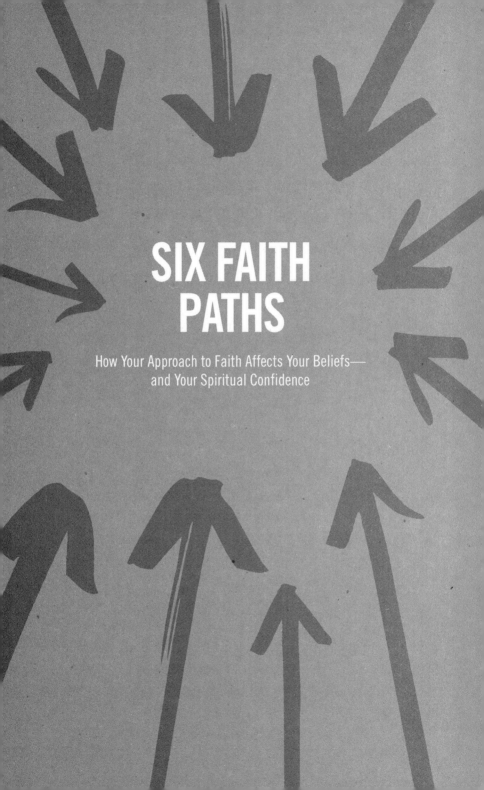

SIX FAITH PATHS

How Your Approach to Faith Affects Your Beliefs—
and Your Spiritual Confidence

CHAPTER TWO

FAITH PATH QUESTIONNAIRE

As we've seen, we all live by at least some measure of faith in regard to our spiritual beliefs. So the important question is this: On what criteria are you basing your beliefs? You've somehow arrived at your current point of view, but how did you get there?

From my observation, we come to our beliefs about God through a variety of approaches—what I've already referred to as the six "faith paths." Knowing which faith path you're on is crucial, because the approach you take can have a huge bearing on what you end up believing as well as on how sure you'll be about those beliefs.

I'm glad that I reassessed the basis of my own faith when I was in college and made sure I was trusting in the right things. It was a vital step in my own journey toward a confident faith, and I think it will be for you, too.

The purpose of this chapter and the "Faith Path Questionnaire" that follows is to help you identify which faith path you've taken to arrive at your current beliefs. Once you've identified your particular path (or paths), the discussions in the chapters that follow will become more helpful to you—especially as you consider not only your own faith path but also which ones your friends and family are now on.

FILLING OUT THE FAITH PATH QUESTIONNAIRE

Here's how to take this simple quiz: read the statements on the following pages and consider the degree to which each one describes you or your beliefs. After reading each statement, write the number that most closely reflects your response. Choose from 0 to 5, according to the following scale:

5 "That's totally me."
4 "That's usually like me."
3 "That's often like me."
2 "That's a little like me."
1 "That's barely like me."
0 "That's not me at all."

Don't spend a lot of time pondering the statements. Simply jot down your initial response, from 0 to 5, and move on to the next one. Repeat the process until you've written down responses to all 42 statements.

_____ 1. What is true for a person depends on his or her particular point of view.

_____ 2. I've never really thought about the reasons for my faith; I just grew up believing it.

_____ 3. It would be unwise to question what I've been taught by my spiritual elders.

_____ 4. Your senses can deceive you; you're better off listening to your heart.

_____ 5. I have confidence in what I believe because God showed me that it's true.

_____ 6. Spiritual teachings need to add up logically; I don't have to fully understand them, but I can't believe anything that contradicts itself.

_____ 7. You shouldn't try to tell someone else what he or she ought to believe.

_____ 8. My beliefs have been clear to me ever since I was taught them as a child.

_____ 9. It makes sense to defer to leaders who have the discernment needed to evaluate spiritual matters.

_____ 10. I can just feel what is right or true.

_____ 11. It may have been through a dream, a vision, or an apparition, but one way or another I received "the message," and I follow it.

_____ 12. People have all kinds of hunches and instincts; if they're not careful, those can get them into a lot of trouble.

_____ 13. Whatever you believe is true for you.

_____ 14. I know many of the words of many of our Scriptures/creeds/doctrines, but not necessarily what they mean.

_____ 15. It would be presumptuous to second-guess what I've been taught; I don't have the knowledge or training needed to make such assessments.

_____ 16. My friends and I talk about spiritual matters and together sense what we should believe.

_____ 17. I know my spiritual direction is right because I often feel God's guiding presence.

_____ 18. I think we should just deal with the facts; it's okay if they fly in the face of conventional thinking.

_____ 19. What matters most is that you are sincere in your beliefs.

_____ 20. I can hardly remember *not* going with my family to worship.

_____ 21. If I don't follow what I've been taught, I will suffer the consequences.

_____ 22. I know what the so-called spiritual experts try to tell us, but I have a hunch they're all wrong.

_____ 23. You can study your books and consult the experts, but God told me what's right, and for me that settles it.

_____ 24. I'd like to believe things people tell me, but I've got to check it out first.

_____ 25. Tolerance means acknowledging that every-one's ideas are true and valuable for them.

_____ 26. I don't think I could ever believe anything other than my religion; our family has practiced it for generations.

_____ 27. I trust the people whose talents, skills, and knowledge have brought them to positions of spiritual influence.

_____ 28. I can usually tell within seconds if something is true.

_____ 29. When our group gets together, we feel God's presence, and that gives us confidence our beliefs are on the right track.

_____ 30. It's easy to glamorize "following your heart" or hanging on to ancient traditions, but what really matters is whether or not something is true.

_____ 31. It would be judgmental to say that my way is right and yours is wrong.

_____ 32. I go to our group's meetings because that's our custom—it's just what we do.

_____ 33. Our book says it, and that settles it.

_____ 34. Generally my mistakes have come when I've ignored my inner guiding voice.

_____ 35. Whether it was an angel, a departed loved one, or some other kind of spiritual being, I can't ignore the insights it gave me.

_____ 36. It's hard to argue with solid evidence.

_____ 37. I can tell something is true by the fact that it's working in my life.

_____ 38. It's hard for me to think about *not* being involved in my particular faith; it's part of my heritage and identity.

_____ 39. It's a high value in my religion to humbly submit to what the leaders say.

_____ 40. I think many people have what might be called a "sixth sense," and they need to pay attention to it.

_____ 41. I didn't know what to think, so I prayed and asked for supernatural guidance—and I was given assurance about which way I should go.

_____ 42. I just try to weigh the information I'm given, carefully consider the source, and reach a logical conclusion.

Now copy the number you wrote by each of the statements to the corresponding blank on the following chart, and total each column. This will help you to see which faith path (or paths) you're currently on—based on the highest score or scores at the bottom of the chart.

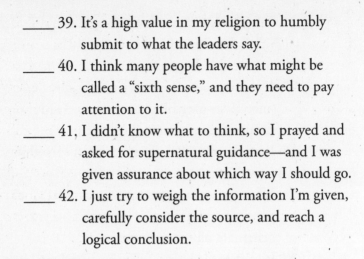

RELATIVISTIC	TRADITIONAL	AUTHORITARIAN	INTUITIVE	MYSTICAL	EVIDENTIAL
1 _____	2 _____	3 _____	4 _____	5 _____	6 _____
7 _____	8 _____	9 _____	10 _____	11 _____	12 _____
13 _____	14 _____	15 _____	16 _____	17 _____	18 _____
19 _____	20 _____	21 _____	22 _____	23 _____	24 _____
25 _____	26 _____	27 _____	28 _____	29 _____	30 _____
31 _____	32 _____	33 _____	34 _____	35 _____	36 _____
37 _____	38 _____	39 _____	40 _____	41 _____	42 _____
TOTAL _____	TOTAL _____	TOTAL _____	TOTAL _____	TOTAL _____	TOTAL _____
DISCUSSED IN CHAPTER 3	DISCUSSED IN CHAPTER 4	DISCUSSED IN CHAPTER 5	DISCUSSED IN CHAPTER 6	DISCUSSED IN CHAPTER 7	DISCUSSED IN CHAPTER 8

What should you do with this information? As you read the six chapters that follow—one per faith path—focus in on the section that corresponds to your primary faith path and consider the advice and encouragement you find there. (If you discover that you're close or equal on two or three faith paths, that's okay. Just give extra attention to those sections and consider the advice that seems to best fit you.) Also, read the other chapters to learn how your friends' and family members' faith paths may be affecting them. And certainly be sure to read chapter 8, on the *Evidential* faith path, to learn how you can become increasingly confident in what you believe.

Some of the advice you'll read may seem challenging to you. There are reasons for that. Socrates said, "The unexamined life is not worth living." It's a very dramatic statement and so highly quotable—but I won't go quite that far. Let me just say that "the unexamined life . . . *is worth examining!*" Because in the process of reassessing your faith path and where it has led you, several important things can happen.

First, you might discover that you've followed weak or faulty reasoning into inadequate or even false beliefs. That's never a pleasant thing to discover—but if it's the case, it's certainly worth finding out as soon as you can. We can all fall into wrong beliefs, but we're wise to detect our error and chart a new course as expeditiously as possible.

Second, you might find out that you've accepted right beliefs, but not for the best of reasons. That was my situation in college. My Christian conclusions were, I'm convinced, correct—but the route I took to get to them was inadequate, so I needed to go back and shore up the foundations underlying my faith.

Third—and this is rare—you might discover that both your approach and your conclusions were spot-on and that all you need to do is reinforce your faith—and then start sharing it with others. If that's you, congratulations; you've started where the rest of us are trying to land. And the result of getting there is that you can be justifiably confident (but never cocky or arrogant) in your faith.

But we won't know which of these situations describes us until we dive into the details of the six faith paths so we can assess where we're currently at and where we need to head next. So let's get on with the journey!

CHAPTER THREE

THE RELATIVISTIC FAITH PATH:

"Truth Is Whatever Works for You"

ATHEIST RICHARD DAWKINS: The onus is on you to say why you believe in something. There's an infinite number of gods you could believe in. I take it you don't believe in Zeus or Apollo or Thor. You believe in presumably the Christian God—

COMMENTATOR BILL O'REILLY: Jesus! Jesus was a real guy, I can see him—

DAWKINS: Yeah—

O'REILLY: I know what he did. And so I'm not positive that Jesus is God, but I'm throwing in with Jesus, rather than throwing in with you guys, because you guys can't tell me how it all got here. You guys don't know.

DAWKINS: We're working on it. Physicists are—

O'REILLY: When you get it, then maybe I'll listen.

DAWKINS: Well now, if you look at the history of science over the centuries, the amount that's gained in knowledge each century is stupendous. In the beginning of the twenty-first century, we don't know everything, we have to be humble. We have to, in humility, say that there's a lot that we still don't know—

O'REILLY: All right, when you guys figure it out, then you come back here and tell me, because until that time I'm sticking with Judeo-Christian philosophy and my religion of Roman Catholicism because it helps me as a person—

DAWKINS: Ah, that's different. If it helps you, that's great. That doesn't mean it's true.

O'REILLY: Well, it's true for me. You see, I believe—

DAWKINS: You mean true for you is different from true for anybody else?

O'REILLY: Yeah, absolutely—

DAWKINS: Something's either got to be true or not!

O'REILLY: No, no. I can't prove to you that Jesus is God, so that truth is mine and mine alone, but you can't prove to me that Jesus is not, so you have to stay in your little belief system.[1]

It was a brief but fascinating exchange on *The O'Reilly Factor* television program between two colorful and outspoken individuals. It also seemed like a classic example of two ships passing in the night. These men were talking to each other in plain English, and they were using the very same word—

truth—but they clearly weren't using the same dictionary to define what they meant by the term.

This question about the nature of truth is a vital one—and coming to grips with it will have a huge bearing on our ability to gain genuine confidence in what we believe. Discussions about this question go back at least as far as the Greek philosophers Plato and Aristotle. The subject came up again during the trial of Jesus, when Pilate, the Roman leader, asked Jesus a seemingly simple question: "What is truth?"[2] We can only wish that Pilate would have waited for a clear answer to his question before walking out of his palace room, because here we are, two thousand years later, still scratching our heads over the very same issue.

Let's think about this. Bill O'Reilly seemed to be claiming that for him, at least in this situation, truth is *what works.* This is what we would call a pragmatic approach. He said, "I'm sticking with Judeo-Christian philosophy and my religion of Roman Catholicism because it helps me as a person. . . . It's true for me. . . . I can't prove to you that Jesus is God, so that truth is mine and mine alone." This set of beliefs is satisfying and seems to be working for O'Reilly, so he declares that it's his own truth.

People talk that way all the time: whatever you believe is "true for you." It's as if we can each have our own private reality. And it's an equal-opportunity way of thinking because, as proponents of this point of view will often tell you, "You have your truth, and I have mine." As long as you're each sincere in your beliefs, the theory goes, and your beliefs are "working for you," then whatever you believe is true for you, even if your so-called truths are contradictory to mine or everyone else's. As one Hollywood screenwriter summed it up, "Whatever the truth is in you . . . you have to be true to *that* truth."[3] The key is that we all just accept each other and our varying "truths"—and simply learn to get along.

This pragmatic, or relativistic, approach to faith is so popular these days that we're highlighting it as the first of the six paths discussed in this book. For simplicity, we'll refer to it as the *Relativistic* faith path.

Sophisticated thinkers will sometimes describe the Relativistic path in terms of differing truths that are based on personal perception and experience. They explain that truth is perspectival. For example, the way you see the world and the way a poor peasant woman in Peru sees the world are going to be completely different. Her truth will be very different from your truth. All of us are limited to our own ideas. Nobody else can see things through your eyes, and you can't see the world through anyone else's eyes. And no one can access the world in a way that gives an objective view, seeing the big picture outside of the limits of our own personal perspectives.

So "truth," according to this approach, is what fits each person's own particular perspective and set of beliefs. As long as something coheres with the rest of your personal understanding of things—your worldview—then it's true for you but not necessarily for anyone else.

Here's one problem with this theory: it speaks authoritatively about the nature of truth, and in so doing presents itself as the one exception that rises above its own rule. In other words, it says that truth is limited to various individuals' points of view, but if that's correct, then the claim itself—that all truth is perspectival—must be limited to the point of view of the person making that claim and thus is not relevant to or binding on the rest of us.

On the other hand, if the Relativistic theory *is* relevant to and binding on the rest of us, then it is the exception that proves that all truth is *not* perspectival. This is a serious, self-defeating contradiction within the Relativistic approach.

Another problem: Have you noticed how often people on the Relativistic path urge others to share their perspective? Maybe you've done it too—possibly hoping to encourage religious tolerance. But when you think about it, that approach is basically trying to move people from their own perspectival positions regarding truth to yours. This reveals an important inconsistency in the theory, namely that the proponents of this view really do believe that at least some ideas and realities are objective enough to allow us to rise above our individual perspectives to see more or less the same thing, in the same way. In other words, some truth isn't relative. Some truth is true for everyone. But this is, again, self-defeating to the entire theory.

That said, the Relativistic path has some good features—in particular, the "getting along" part. I'm all for tolerance of other people's beliefs. I'll fight for the civil rights of the wide spectrum of religions and spiritual practices—including ones that might seem strange or even a bit wacky to me—as long as they're not breaking laws or overtly hurting people. In that sense I agree with the idea that we need to "Coexist," as the ubiquitous bumper sticker puts it.

I also believe in letting each person practice his or her own faith, with the hope that in the marketplace of ideas the more worthwhile ones will rise to the top. It's part of what

I love about Western culture—the freedom to think about and weigh ideas and to decide for ourselves. But let's be clear: supporting the legal rights of a wide gamut of religions and "-isms" is not the same as thinking they're all *true*. It's simply acknowledging that we see things differently, while still agreeing to be good neighbors, to care about one another, and to listen to one another's points of view. And maybe even learn some things along the way.

Religious tolerance is a very good thing; but saying that *everybody's beliefs are true* is, in my mind, completely incoherent.

Let me illustrate why that is. If I try to apply the relativistic theories of "*what works* for me is true" or "*what fits* for me is true" directly to the O'Reilly/Dawkins dialogue, I would have to conclude that, for Richard Dawkins, God really does not exist, because Dawkins doesn't believe in him. But at the same time, and in an equally real way, the Christian God *does* exist for Bill O'Reilly, because O'Reilly sincerely believes in that God.

Do you see the problem? Under this scenario, God does and does not exist at the same time, for two different people, based on their own particular beliefs. Now, I believe that God can to do amazing miracles—but pulling off simultaneous existence and nonexistence seems like a stretch, even for the Almighty.

And if we add to the conversation a Hindu, who believes that the entire material world is illusory maya and is just part of the mind of the pantheistic One, then for him *everything* is God. This includes Dawkins and O'Reilly, the chairs they're sitting on, the air they're breathing, and so forth. It's all part of the all-encompassing, impersonal god, whom we can't know, and who can't know us.

So if this Hindu enters the room with Dawkins and O'Reilly, then god/God has to pull off an even more amazing feat: not existing at all (the atheist perspective); existing as the personal, creator God (in Christian terms); and existing as the impersonal All (the Hindu concept). All three, all at once. And I won't even try to explain what happens when a Scientologist enters the room!

I think my explanation was fair to the views of each party—including the relativist who claims to hold to this kind of a multi-truth "understanding." And as much as it might seem tempting to try to be "politically correct" by saying that everyone in the scenario is right, I just can't bring myself to play that kind of mind game.

Now let me weigh in on this question myself. Going back to the dialogue we started with, I'm afraid I have to side with Richard Dawkins, the atheist, this time around. Not on his final conclusions about God, of course, but on his seemingly clearer and stronger definition of truth, which he stated so simply when he said, "Something's either got to be true or not!"

Call me old fashioned, but truth is just what's real. Not my own private reality—or yours—but the way things actually are. Truth is *what is*—what exists really exists, and what doesn't exist really doesn't exist—whether we like it or not, whether we can prove it or not, whether we have different perceptions about it, or whether we think about it or believe in it at all.

Maybe a few everyday examples will help (though you'll just have to go with me on the first one). Let's say you don't believe in trucks. You've heard about trucks, you've known people who claimed to own a truck, and you've talked to people who say they've ridden in trucks. You've even seen artists' renditions of trucks as well as alleged photographs of them. The evidence for trucks sometimes seems pretty strong—but you're still not convinced. "It's all part of a vast and extremely clever truck-cult conspiracy," you say, "because there actually are no trucks."

Then you decide to cross the street. You look to the left and you look to the right. No cars are coming. No motorcycles or bikes either. Not even a horse-drawn buggy. However, there is something that looks very much like a truck barreling down the road toward you. But this doesn't fool you, because, of course, you know that trucks don't exist. So you step off the curb and onto the pavement—right into the path of what you are sure is the deceptive but harmless apparition of a nonexistent truck.

So here's the question: Will your sincerely held "anti-truck" beliefs save you from the reality of the twenty-ton semi that is about to impose its very real existence on your oh-so-vulnerable body? Of course not! Your *what fits* disbelief is about to encounter genuine *what is* reality, and like it or not, your conspiracy theories and skepticism about trucks aren't going to make a whit of difference. Reality is just that way—harsh, but so very real. Soon you'll be *wearing* that truck, or vice versa.

I have a friend who likes to chide his relativist buddies for getting up in the morning and routinely drinking a glass of orange juice before leaving the house to do other activities, such as filling their cars with gasoline. "If reality is really relative to what you believe it to be," he says, "then why don't you reverse your morning routine, and drink a glass of gasoline before you fill your car with orange juice?" It seems silly, yes, but if relativism were true and the person were actually sincere in his belief that gasoline is good for humans and orange juice is good for cars, then it should all work out fine. I'm sure it won't surprise you to know that my friend hasn't had any takers on his suggestion.

Or how about this: next time you're on a road trip that takes you down Interstate 110, decide in your mind that *what works* for you is to interpret the 110 number on the highway sign as the speed limit. Don't do this haphazardly. Really be sincere in your belief that this is the case, knowing it works for you and fits your broader belief that automobile manufacturers install speedometers that go up to 160 miles per hour for good reason—and then simply step on the accelerator. It'll be a wild and exciting ride, and you might get to your destination sooner than expected.

Oh, but be ready to explain to the officer who pulls you over that *what fits* within your belief system is that the speed limit is 110 miles per hour. When he sees your sincerity and understands that this is *what works* for you, I'm sure he'll just smile and send you on your way. Do you think? Or do you suppose he might hold you to his own truth—the *real* truth of the actual speed limit of 65 miles per hour—and hand you a stout speeding ticket? If you're not sure of the answer you could always try it for yourself . . . but be ready to pay a hefty price!

Or one more: a family member comes home late one night, looking a little disheveled and acting a bit sheepish, smelling of alcohol and in no mood to talk. When you ask what's going on, what kind of answer do you hope to get back? Would you be satisfied with a *what works* response, or are you looking for a true, *what is* answer?

Keep in mind that the *what works* approach to truth could lead him or her to say whatever you want to hear so that you'll let up and not probe any deeper. If it keeps you off the warpath, then that's *what works* at that moment. That's enough "truth" for one night.

Can you see why it's the old-fashioned understanding of truth (the authentic *what is* variety) that we really want and need to live our lives by—and that we expect others around us to live by, as well? That's the view of truth that Plato, Aristotle, Jesus, and most good thinkers have held through the ages—and it's certainly the one that we try to hold people to in our courts of law.

Our job in all of the examples above, and in any others I can imagine, is to avoid inventing a fantasy version of reality within our own minds—one we then hope will materialize and somehow magically become real. (If you think about it, that's a pretty good description of *delusion*.) Instead, we must find out what *truly* is real, and then align our lives and actions to that reality.

Trucks really do exist and can run you over—so you'd be wise not to step out in front of one. Orange juice is good to drink, but gasoline can kill you—so choose your beverages carefully. The sign that says 110 on the interstate is telling you the route number, not the speed limit—and the officer in that car with the red-and-blue flashing lights will hold you accountable for understanding and abiding by the actual speed limit, whether you call yourself a relativist or otherwise. And family members who come home three sheets to the wind need to provide a truthful explanation—one that corresponds with the facts.

This all seems pretty obvious, don't you think? It does, at least, until we approach the world of *spiritual matters*. Many people apply commonsense thinking to ordinary, concrete situations, like the examples above. But when it comes to beliefs about spiritual matters, they quickly revert to relativistic modes of thinking.

Why is that? Why is it that a smart guy like Bill O'Reilly can be such a hard-nosed realist about things like politics, legal issues, and cultural controversies, yet revert so quickly to a subjective, *what works* approach to truth when he talks about his religious faith?

One reason is that religious faith deals in the realm of the invisible—of things we can't see, touch, or feel—including God and the supernatural. These realities are harder to verify. We can't completely prove or disprove them, so we often allow ourselves to get mushy in how we think and talk about them. We unwittingly begin to play mind games, saying things like, "God can exist for me but not for you—and that's okay, because we're both entitled to our own truth." We talk as if religious ideas are some kind of therapeutic projection that is designed to make us feel better but is not based on anything real. I'll take an aspirin; you take a placebo—as long as we both feel better, who cares which one was the real medicine?

If that's the way you came to your faith, it's easy to lose confidence in it. What if believing in Jesus works for you today, but stops working tomorrow? What if Christianity is true this week, but there's no certainty it will be true next week?

But truth isn't like that. Not in the physical realm and not in the spiritual realm either. In both areas, *what is* really is. Whatever is real in the spiritual realm was already real before we arrived. And it will remain that way, whether or not we think about it, believe or disbelieve it, or ignore it altogether.

So if Bill O'Reilly turns out to be right about the Christian God in a real *what is* kind of way, then that same God exists for Richard Dawkins and everyone else, even if Dawkins writes a hundred books against him. By the same token, if Richard Dawkins turns out to be right in a real *what is* kind of way about the nonexistence of God, then the singing of hymns, the praying of prayers, and the sincere beliefs of you, me, or Bill O'Reilly won't make some kind of God pop into existence.

Reality is just what is. Truth, even truth about spiritual realities, is not produced by what we decide to believe in. What's real already exists, with or without our belief in it; we just need to discover what it is and then conform our beliefs to it.

Also, I've already alluded to this, but let me state it clearly: sincerity doesn't change reality. You can join a mushroom cult, but your deeply trusted, sincerely felt beliefs that Jesus was a mushroom aren't going to make him into a mushroom. Sincerity may be admirable, but let's be honest: *you can be sincere but sincerely wrong.*

And let's be honest about something else, too. Nobody *really* believes that "every religion is true." That's the kind of thing people say when they're pretty sure nobody's going to press them on it. The truth is, we all draw lines in the sand somewhere.

Don't believe me? Then why aren't *you* a member of the mushroom cult? It actually does exist, and they really do think that Jesus was some kind of a highly evolved mushroom. (And you thought I was making this stuff up. Welcome to the weird world of religious cults!)

Or what about the Heaven's Gate UFO group? Remember those folks who moved to California, rented a mansion, put on uniforms that included the now infamous black-and-white running shoes, lay side by side on bunk beds, and then poisoned themselves—all so they'd be freed from their bodies and ready to be picked up by a soon-to-be-arriving spaceship they thought was flying behind the comet Hale-Bopp as it neared the earth? Sad as the outcome was, the word *wacky* isn't too strong for this one, wouldn't you agree?

Or remember the horrific events surrounding the Jim Jones cult, in which his flock of nearly a thousand people in Guyana drank cyanide-laced Flavor Aid in order to escape scrutiny and prosecution? And what about David Koresh and his group of followers who allowed their compound in Waco, Texas, to burn to the ground—with themselves and their families all inside?

I think we'd acknowledge that at least these particular belief systems were wrong—even though the people in them may have been completely sincere. If so, then we're in agreement: not every religion is true. When differing groups teach contradictory ideas about God, faith, and spiritual matters, they simply can't all be right—they can't all represent *what is*.

Here's one more reason we can't accept the idea that everybody's "truth" is valid: deep down, we all think *we're* right and anyone who disagrees with us is wrong. And if you disagree with that statement, you've only illustrated my point!

None of this, of course, proves who is actually right concerning their views of God. It simply lays out some essential ground rules: we must look for genuine truth and reality, the kind that accurately describes *what is*—even in the areas we can't see. Only then will we possess a confident faith.

Where should we start? First, we need to cling to what's real. As the Old Testament Scriptures put it, we need to "love truth."[4] Being a lover of truth takes persistence—and a certain degree of mental toughness. We have to be willing to seek and accept what is actually the case, even if it flies in the face of what we've thought in the past or what we wish for in the present.

I like the attitude of some of the early Greek philosophers who engaged in debates over truth. Some, I'm told, would tell the audience at the outset of the debate that the best thing that could happen would be for the opposing debater to win. Why? Because in the process the first debater and his supporters would be helped to better see, understand, and accept truth. Discussions conducted with this mind-set were not "a contest between opponents . . . but a cooperative search for truth and understanding."[5]

So let's follow this example. If the Relativistic path led you to faith in Jesus, that's wonderful! But if you want to be really confident that you've chosen a faith that is true and will last, it's time to move off the Relativistic faith path. (If the Relativistic path has led you to a different conclusion, my challenge is the same.) Let's stop placing our faith in *what works* and instead tenaciously track down what's really true. (To learn more about this, read chapter 8, which discusses the *Evidential* faith path.) And once we've discovered *what is*, let's be willing to take the courageous step of aligning our beliefs and actions to the truth we've discovered.

CHAPTER FOUR

THE TRADITIONAL FAITH PATH:

"Truth Is What You've Always Been Taught"

I lived in Southern California for most of the past decade.

I know—it's regarded by the rest of the country, and perhaps by much of the world, as a land of quirky health fads and eccentric people. I don't take that personally, even if I do remember spending thirty-eight dollars one day at Trader Joe's—and then realizing as the cashier was bagging my purchases that I had just blown two twenties on nothing but fresh fruits and raw nuts. I guess I was pretty well acclimated to SoCal culture.

Where else could you go swimming, hiking, or mountain biking virtually every day—about fifty weeks a year? I recall one day when I was out riding my bike. I was pedaling up a long hill, doing some serious sweating, and thinking to myself how I wished it weren't so hot out—and then I felt guilty when I realized it was *February*.

I liked that we could ski in the morning on the snowy slopes of the San Bernardino Mountains, and then on the afternoon of the same day, after a short drive, swim along the sun-drenched shores of the Pacific Ocean. (I never actually did this. I just enjoyed knowing that I could.)

People in Orange County decorate their palm trees for the holidays. You just had to smile, seeing lights and tinsel hanging from the tropical foliage. I even knew a guy who each Christmas would turn on his air conditioner to its highest setting and wait until it got really cold in the house. Then he would light the fireplace, and he and his family would put on warm sweaters and sit around shivering together, pretending that it was, like, real winter!

Heidi and I—along with our kids, Emma Jean and Matthew—really did love our years living there, in what felt to us almost like paradise on earth.

So why was it that every year when the holidays rolled around, I started to feel homesick? I know that probably seems like a normal impulse to you—until you realize where the home I was longing for actually was . . . *North Dakota*.

Nothing against my beloved home state or any of my family or friends who live there—it was a great place to grow up, and the people are wonderful—but have you ever *been* to North Dakota? Probably not. It's one of the least-visited tourist states in the Union. Why? Two major problems.

First, the state is simply not on the way to anywhere. Unless you need to drive from Bemidji, Minnesota, to Big Sky, Montana, or perhaps take a trek from Sioux Falls, South

Dakota, to Saskatoon, Saskatchewan, you're not likely to venture into NoDak territory. If you want to get there, you've got to be intentional about it. Not to mention that few airlines actually operate there, and for the price of a ticket you might have been able to fly to Paris or Prague.

Second, there's the Winter Weather (yes, it's so intense it must be capitalized). My brother-in-law, Glen, who lives twenty-three miles from the Canadian border, describes it like this: "We have nine months of winter, and then we have three months of really bad snowmobiling." The week Heidi and I got married in her hometown of Velva, which is sort of a suburb of my hometown of Minot, the windchill got all the way down to ninety degrees below zero. Can you imagine? We *had* to get married—just to stay warm!

I discovered the ultimate symbol of a North Dakota winter one day when my father-in-law, Hillis, was visiting our home in California and I noticed some scratches on the tops of his leather walking shoes. "Hillis," I asked, "what happened to your new shoes?" Matter-of-factly he replied, "Oh, those are from the chains I clamp on when I'm at home, so I can go for walks through the snow and ice." *Of course*, I thought, as shivers went up my spine.

I think you're getting my point: North Dakota is a cold, out-of-the-way place—one that most people would rather avoid during winter months. And yet, I *still* got strangely homesick for it around the holidays. It got so bad at times that I would come really close to throwing the entire family into the car—spur of the moment—along with all the Christmas gifts, parkas, sweaters, scarves and gloves, boots, tire chains, and even the dog. All so we could abandon the eighty-degree California weather to risk our lives and drive almost two thousand miles through the desert, over the mountains, and onto the ice-packed highways straight into the tundra in order to get to my parents' and my in-laws' houses in time for the holidays.

Thankfully, I'd come to my senses just in the nick of time, put another string of lights on the palm tree, pour myself a glass of eggnog, and settle for simply calling our snowbound relatives instead. But one thing's for sure: tradition is a powerful magnet. Especially when that tradition involves the place we call *home*.

One of the most haunting pieces of literature I've ever read is a short story called "The Lottery," written by Shirley Jackson in the late 1940s. The basic story line is this: in a small, old-fashioned, and seemingly friendly town of about three hundred people, they have an annual practice that goes back further than anyone can remember. The residents gather together at the same time each year, and the head of each household draws a piece of paper out of a splintered, old, black wooden box. Because it's a small, close-knit community, they know exactly how many families will be part of the lottery. They put just the right number of pieces of paper in the box—all blank, except one, which has a black spot on it.

The unfortunate family that draws the piece of paper with the spot on it then has to bring every member of their household, from youngest to oldest—small children included—back up to the box to draw pieces of paper, again with just one piece having the spot on it. This time, whichever unlucky soul happens to get the marked piece of paper is immediately turned upon by the entire crowd—every man, woman, and child, including the victim's own family—and is summarily stoned to death.

In the story, Tessie Hutchinson, a beloved and respected community member, wife of Bill Hutchinson, and mother of three, draws the ill-fated ballot. The tale ends as she screams, "It isn't fair! It isn't right!"

And then, we're told, the townspeople "were upon her."

What's interesting is that the characters don't even question why they do this horrible thing each year. But when a man named Mr. Adams mentions to a senior townsman called Old Man Warner that "over in the north village they're thinking of giving up the lottery," Warner's stern response gives a hint of the superstition that backs up the town's terrible tradition.

"Pack of crazy fools," he replies. "Listening to the young folks, nothing's good enough for them. Next thing you know, they'll be wanting to go back to living in caves, nobody work anymore, live that way for a while. Used to be a saying about 'Lottery in June, corn be heavy soon.' First thing you know, we'd all be eating stewed chickweed and acorns. *There's always been a lottery.*"[1]

As frightening as that fictional story is, it illustrates a sobering truth about traditions. They're just habits, sometimes older than memory, and they're often accepted without question or even real thought. "Why challenge it?" the reasoning goes. "It's the way we've always done things around here."

Traditions can be positive, like an old family custom or surroundings that make you feel at home—or practices like giving supplies to people who are in need around the holidays.

Traditions can also be neutral—neither helpful nor harmful—like the story of the woman who cooked a Sunday roast each week for her family. Before putting the roast in the pan she would always cut the ends off of the meat. One time, as she was doing this, her daughter asked, "Mom, why do you cut off the edges of the roast before you put it in the pan?" Her answer: "Well, that's just what you have to do." But the girl persisted. "Why? Does it make it taste better or cook more evenly?" she asked. "I really don't know; it's just what Grandma always did. I do it that way because it's what she taught me. When we visit her, let's ask her why."

So the next time they were at the grandmother's house they asked her why she always trimmed the ends off the roasts before putting them in the oven. Puzzled, she said, "I don't do that." Surprised, the mother insisted, "Yes, you do, and that's what you taught me to do years ago when you first showed me how to prepare a roast."

"Oh," the grandmother replied with a chuckle, "I used to have to do that because back then I had such a small pan—it was the only way I could make a large roast fit into it."

Funny story, but funnier still how many things we do in our daily lives that are like that. "Well, that's just what you have to do," we reassure ourselves.

Traditions can also be negative and yet be passed down just as blindly as any other. Certainly that was the case in "The Lottery," but it's often that way in real life as well.

Many of our forebears, for example, used to make demeaning remarks about people of different skin color, or they'd lump together certain ethnic groups under one derogatory banner. They didn't necessarily intend to be mean; they were simply passing on the stereotypes they had picked up from their friends and relatives. "Oh, it's best that those folks stick together with their own kind, on their own side of town," they'd say. "Some of them can be nice enough as people, but you wouldn't want them living in your neighborhood or attending your house of worship." And they might add, "Just watch out if you ever have to do business with one of them. You've got to watch 'em like a hawk."

These ugly prejudices get passed on, generation to generation. About the time we think we're finally free of them, an old label or expression will come up somewhere in a conversation, and we realize that this is one tradition we must continually and tenaciously work to root out.

Another negative tradition some of us had handed down was the habit of smoking several packs of cigarettes a day. Years ago this was considered fashionable, a way to fit in, and the cigarettes didn't cost much back then either. Why not light up like everyone else? Then, as more and more people got sick, and mounting evidence suggested that these "cancer sticks" really can kill you, smoking proved to be a very hard habit to break. Some of us lost our grandparents prematurely as a result. Unfortunately, many of our parents "inherited" their harmful nicotine habits, and even after the avalanche of incriminating evidence came out about the devastating impact of using tobacco, many from my generation—and the next—still find themselves addicted today.

The same kind of generational hand-me-down habits are seen in a variety of other damaging areas:

- alcohol and drug addictions
- negative attitudes toward people of different religions or gender
- poor and sometimes destructive communication patterns
- tendencies toward overworking and under-resting
- parental neglect of children
- unhealthy eating and exercise habits
- abusiveness between family members

We should respect our elders but also step back and make an honest assessment of their habits and lifestyles before we lock into their patterns of thinking. We need to candidly ask ourselves, "How did their beliefs and actions work out for them? Do I want to see similar results in my own life?"

If we're to resist passing down through the generations what my friend Bill Hybels calls "a broken baton" of harmful habits, beliefs, and attitudes, then we'll have to pause and consider our own lives very carefully—and probably make some challenging course corrections along the way.

Nowhere in our lives is a critical evaluation more needed than in the area of *faith*. Most of us grew up with some kind of inherited belief system, whether Christian or otherwise. If we've passively accepted what we've been taught as sort of a hand-me-down religion, then we have, knowingly or unknowingly, signed up for the *Traditional* faith path. It is the most common approach people use to "choose" their beliefs—though it's usually not a choice at all.

One way or another, you were initiated, baptized, consigned, or commissioned into a particular set of religious beliefs (even if it's the beliefs of atheism, which some practice quite religiously). Today you might wear the label of whatever group those beliefs represent, but if pressed, you couldn't give a compelling reason for why you think you're in the right faith. For you, it's just a tradition—which might explain why you sometimes have felt halfhearted and noncommittal about your beliefs.

Now, that doesn't necessarily make the faith you grew up with wrong or bad. In fact, chances are that at least some elements of what you've been raised to believe are helpful and true. But if you got your faith as a hand-me-down, then it's sort of the luck of the draw. If you think about it, you're just banking on the hope that somewhere back in your family history, somebody carefully examined the whole realm of questions about God, spirituality, and *what is* before coming to a conclusion about faith.

But that's a huge roll of the dice. Because these are the same people who were working sixty or eighty hours a week in order to get by; moving from place to place trying to find a better life; learning new cultures and maybe even a new language; and perhaps (going back to our earlier list) trying to overcome their inbred prejudices, struggling with various addictions, fighting with other family members or factions of society, and so forth. How much time and energy do you think they were able to carve out for serious reflection about spiritual realities?

The answer is that they probably didn't give this vitally important area nearly the focus it deserves—and maybe not even as much, going back to chapter 1, as I gave to researching and buying my mountain bike. And yet, far too readily, we're prone to accept what they handed down to us as being absolute, gospel truth.

We must beware of turning our traditions—or our family background, heritage, culture, or ethnicity—into an excuse to blindly perpetuate something that may or may not be healthy, helpful, or even true. The philosophy of "that's just what you have to do" simply doesn't cut it when it comes to embracing a faith you can confidently live with over the long haul.

My philosopher friend Paul Copan, who is an expert in these matters, was asked whether we aren't culturally conditioned to just accept and live with the beliefs we grew up with, regardless of what they are. The question was posed to him like this: "Isn't it true that if you were born in Saudi Arabia, you'd probably be a Muslim, or if you were born in India, you'd probably be a Hindu?"

"Statistically speaking, that could be true," Copan replied. "And if the pluralist had grown up in medieval France or modern Somalia, he probably wouldn't be a pluralist. So the geography argument doesn't carry much weight. Besides, I could make the claim that if you lived in Nazi Germany, the chances are you would have been part of the Hitler Youth. Or if you lived in Stalin's Russia, you would have been a Communist. But does that mean Nazism or Communism is as good a political system as democracy?

"No—just because there has been a diversity of political

systems through history' doesn't prevent us from concluding that one political system is superior to its rivals. Presumably, there are good reasons for preferring one political system over another. There are good reasons for rejecting a system like Nazism or Communism in favor of democracies. So why can't it be the same with regard to religious beliefs?

"The point is: are there good reasons for believing one religious viewpoint over another?"[2]

It's interesting that Jesus, the greatest teacher of all time, was also perhaps the hardest on tradition. Listen to his surprisingly stinging words, aimed at the spiritual authorities of his day and recorded in one of four early biographies:

> *The Pharisees and teachers of religious law asked him,*
> *"Why don't your disciples follow our age-old tradition?*
> *They eat without first performing the hand-washing*
> *ceremony."*
> *Jesus replied, "You hypocrites! Isaiah was right when*
> *he prophesied about you, for he wrote,*
> *'These people honor me with their lips,*
> *   but their hearts are far from me.*
> *Their worship is a farce,*
> *   for they teach man-made ideas as commands*
> *   from God.'*
> *For you ignore God's law and substitute your own*
> *tradition."[3]*

If you read this story in its surrounding context, you'll see that Jesus was so incensed with the Pharisees and teachers of the law that he repeated his indictment against blindly following tradition three times in one short conversation. Apparently, he saw the spiritual devastation that resulted from blindly following the beliefs and edicts of earlier generations, and he wanted to jolt his listeners into a more careful consideration of these matters. For him, it was much more important to get it right than to keep the peace, gloss over problems, or fit into familial or cultural expectations. And interestingly, he was echoing prior warnings given centuries earlier through the prophet Isaiah, who wrote, "The Lord says, 'These people say they are mine. They honor me with their lips, but their hearts are far from me. And their worship of me is nothing but man-made rules learned by rote.'"[4]

So the question for us is this: Are we willing to step back and examine our inherited beliefs and make sure that we've thoughtfully and intentionally adopted a faith worth following?

Here's the point we need to grapple with: our parents could have been wrong! And their parents could have been wrong before them. And our religious leaders and teachers might also have been wrong.

Looking at things more broadly, *somebody's* parents and teachers *must* be wrong. Why? Because so many contradict each other. As we know, and as we'll discuss further in an upcoming chapter, opposites cannot both be true. This "law of noncontradiction" is an inescapable reality—and you can't even argue about it without implicitly agreeing with it. (I say this because you can't dispute the laws of logic without employing the very same laws. In fact, you can't even *think* about disputing the laws of logic without using them.)

Applying this principle of noncontradiction to matters of faith means that the personal God of Christianity is not compatible with the impersonal Brahma of Hinduism. Either God is an intelligent deity, who is distinct from the universe that he made, or he is an unconscious and impersonal pantheistic god, who is in and part of everything—but he can't be *both* in any meaningful sense. Logically, both concepts could be wrong, of course, but they can't both be right, because they are incompatible and contradictory.

As we said earlier, we should support the legal right of both of these traditions (and others) to exist and to spread their messages. That's *tolerance*, which is great. But don't confuse tolerance with *truth*. There can't be two contradictory-but-true realities in the sense of genuine, *what is* truth.

To be fair, I had to face this same reality myself—as I mentioned—when I was in my philosophy class. "Truths" that I had been raised to believe and that I had always considered to be rock solid were being challenged by a professor who seemed to know more about the subject than most of the spiritual teachers and influencers in my life. I sensed that I was no match for this challenge, and the people I talked to about it at my church weren't much help either. So what was I to do?

When faced with the possibility that something you've been taught all your life might actually be wrong—as I did in college—it's tempting to try various defense maneuvers as a means of justifying and clinging to your traditions. Avoidance is one of those tactics—doing all you can to get away from the influence that is causing you to question. Maybe if you don't think about it, or don't get near that person or place— maybe if you just put a pillow over your head—the threat will disappear. But then the problem is left to fester beneath the surface, causing doubt and insecurity to spread like a cancer. I've met people whose faith was challenged years earlier, but who never addressed the issues adequately. Their confidence was still weakened, even after the passing of so much time.

Other people respond by getting indignant or angry: "Who are you to say that your way is right and mine is wrong? How arrogant!" Such a reaction might feel good at first—but in the end the questions still linger. And deep down you know that it really is possible that the other person's beliefs could be right—and that you have been taught things that are wrong (even though they were sincerely believed by your parents or others who influenced you).

Wouldn't it be freeing to just relax and decide that you would rather be a lover of truth than merely a defender of a tradition? Wouldn't you rather know that you are sincerely seeking an accurate picture of spiritual realities and building your beliefs on ideas that are supported by the facts?

You see, traditional beliefs can be a wonderful thing, both for you and for those you pass them down to—but only insofar as they are actually based on truth. So the testing of the tradition can serve you in one of two beneficial ways: either you'll find out it's based of falsehood and myth, and thus have the liberty to set it aside and find something better to believe in; or you'll discover that there is a real foundation of truth underlying those traditional teachings, and end up confirming that this is something to hold on to. Either way, you win—and end up with a set of beliefs you can embrace and pass on wholeheartedly to the next generation.

Ultimately what we're recommending is the very thing the Bible admonishes us to do in 1 Thessalonians 5:21, where it tells us to "test everything. . . . Hold on to what is good."

You don't need to become a spiritual iconoclast, challenging every authority or discarding every tradition. Rather, you should maintain respect for your family and teachers while simultaneously scrutinizing what they've taught you. Recognize that most of us start out with beliefs that were handed down to us, and it's a natural part of growing into adulthood to step back and evaluate the validity of the ideas you've inherited. You simply need to decide to weigh the reasons and evidence for what you have accepted up to now—so you can be confident that you'll end up with a faith that really makes sense because it's based on actual truth.

That was the course of action I took in college. To the best of my ability, I lowered my defenses, opened my mind, and began a process of examining the very foundations of the beliefs I had been taught. And frankly, it was an uncomfortable season for me.

So for a time I lived with a sense of spiritual disequilibrium, while I vigorously went to work reading books, listening to recorded talks, researching answers, and interacting with wise people who could contribute to my understanding. I thoroughly tested my traditions with logic, evidence, and frequent prayers for guidance, trusting that the truth would make itself clear.

This process led me eventually to a wealth of helpful information, and it ultimately served to deepen my Christian faith. In hindsight, the doubts and challenges I wrestled with proved to be like infections that produced "spiritual antibodies" in me as I studied and responded to them. In the end, I was stronger for having undergone this time of searching, probing, and testing, and I was therefore more confident in the faith I'd embraced—though this result was certainly not guaranteed at the outset.

For my friend Lee Strobel, the opposite happened. He had come to accept a worldview that was secular, skeptical, and had no room for God. He was a spiritual doubter who, over time, began to reexamine—and eventually to doubt—his own doubts. The catalyst for this change was the example set by his wife, Leslie, who, after coming to faith in God, gently challenged Lee to take another look at what he believed.

His initial reaction to this process was to get angry. He slammed doors, belittled his wife's newfound faith, lashed out against her church, and increased his use and abuse of alcohol. One day, in his frustration, he even kicked a hole in their living room wall.

Gradually, though, Lee settled down and opened up to reason and truth, instead of simply reacting emotionally. To this day, he'll tell you that he did not enjoy having his atheistic traditions challenged. And he didn't relish the thought of acknowledging a God who, once allowed through the door, would have a say in how he lived his life.

But somehow Lee found the humility—and the persistence—to wrestle with his spiritual questions, to examine the purported answers, and to carefully weigh the evidence, both pro and con. It took him nearly two years. In the end, instead of reaffirming his atheistic faith, he had a complete change of mind. Or, as he now puts it, he experienced "a rush of reason." Leslie Strobel describes it more as a miraculous change of heart. Today, Lee is a devout Christian, and he writes books and speaks to groups all over the world, helping others who are on spiritual journeys similar to his own.[5]

I don't know where your journey will take you. It could be a reaffirmation of the teachings and traditions you grew up with, as it was for me. Or it could be a redirection of your thinking toward a fresh set of beliefs, as it was for Lee. But I'll tell you one thing for certain: both Lee and I are glad we embarked on the adventure of spiritual discovery. We're thankful we did what it took to examine our beliefs and to carefully and deliberately find a faith we could count on. (To learn how you can do the same thing, read chapter 8, which discusses the *Evidential* faith path.)

The only way you will be truly confident about your faith will be to test your traditions—to make sure that they are grounded in truth.

CHAPTER FIVE

THE AUTHORITARIAN FAITH PATH:

"Truth Is What You've Been Told You Must Believe"

It was a first for me. I had never been inside a mosque before, and neither had most of the people who were taking the tour with me. We were cordially welcomed, shown around the premises, and then ushered into a large room and asked to sit down on the floor.

Soon the imam, dressed in white, stepped to the front of the room and began to speak to us. He passionately communicated with a strong, confident voice. He explained some of the central tenets of Islam, and then he described how Muslims pray, worship in the mosque, and live out their faith in daily life.

Then his gaze grew intense—even stern—as he addressed some issues pertinent to Christians. "It is important for you to know that Allah is the one and only God, and that Muhammad, peace be upon him, was his true prophet. God is not divided, and he does not have a son," he declared emphatically. "Jesus, peace be upon him, was *not* the Son of God. He was a true prophet, like Muhammad, and we are to honor him—but we must never worship him. We worship Allah and Allah alone."

He went on speaking to our group a bit longer, wrapped up his comments, and then said he'd be willing to take some questions. People asked about a variety of topics, some surface-level and others more substantive. The imam patiently responded to each one. As I listened, I wrestled silently with some matters I was sure would go to the heart of what he had said and to the core of the difference between his faith and my own.

I knew that Islamic teachings say that Jesus not only was not the Son of God but also never even made such a claim. Further, they declare that Jesus did not die on the cross, because, as I've heard Muslims explain it, "God would never allow one of his prophets to face such shame and disgrace." Also, because they don't believe in the crucifixion of Jesus, they obviously don't believe in the resurrection claims about him either. I felt compelled to bring up these issues, so I raised my hand to ask my question.

"I'm curious about something," I said. "Jesus' followers walked and talked with him for several years. They also reported that he repeatedly claimed to be the Son of God, that they watched him die on the cross, and that three days later they saw and talked and ate with him after his resurrection. We have detailed accounts of what they heard and saw.

These have been preserved in literally thousands of manuscript documents that attest to these realities.

"So we have all of this written testimony from the people who were companions of Jesus, each affirming that he claimed to be the Son of God, died on a cross, and rose from the dead. Now, correct me if I'm wrong, but what Islam teaches us about Jesus seems to be based on the words of one man, Muhammad, who, six hundred years after the time of Christ, was sitting in a cave when, as he claimed, an angel spoke to him and told him these things weren't so.

"What I'm curious about is whether you have any historical or logical reasons why we should accept that viewpoint over and against the actual historical record?"

The imam looked at me intently. After a pause, he declared resolutely, *"I choose to believe the prophet!"*—and the discussion was over.

Honestly, that sounded to me a lot like "I've got my mind made up, so don't confuse me with the facts." For him, the influences of his religion and its founder were all he needed. He seemed like an intelligent person, but if he had deeper reasons backing up his commitment to his faith, he had chosen not to share them.

Very few people arrive at their particular spiritual point of view through careful evaluation of the logic and evidence supporting it. Most accept it either because they grew up with it (as we discussed in the previous chapter, concerning the Traditional faith path) or because influential people in their lives expect and even demand it of them—whether they be devout Muslims; Jehovah's Witnesses who go door-to-door tirelessly talking about God's theocratic kingdom; North Koreans who worship and revere their deceased "Great Leader," Kim Il Sung; or even some Christians who feel compelled by powerful teachers to "stay true to the Lord" by obeying their commands, whether those commands make sense to them or not.

This approach to choosing your beliefs is what I call the *Authoritarian* faith path. It is similar to the Traditional faith path in that it's hard to call it a "choice," because it's usually passively received. But the difference between the two is that the Traditional approach is more about a *habit* that gets passed on from one generation to the next, whereas the Authoritarian approach is based on *submission* to a religious leader—past or present—and the ideas that leader holds up as the standard to live by.

Like many people, you may have grown up under some sort of religious authority, and when you were younger you just naturally accepted what you were taught without critically analyzing it. But part of reaching maturity in these matters is to come to the point where you step back and take a more careful look. You say to yourself, "This might have seemed right in my life up until now—but I need to examine who and what it is that I'm following to see if they warrant my ongoing trust and loyalty."

It's interesting that the original meaning of the Arabic word *Islam* is actually "submission," and it seems fair to say that many Muslims accept their faith primarily by submitting to the authority of their parents, teachers, government, or society. Some, I'm sure, have stepped back and tried to examine whether what they've been taught is true—but the message that is most often communicated, in my observation, is an authoritative declaration that Allah is the true God, Muhammad is his messenger, and you need to submit yourself to these realities. The imam did not say to me that day, "I've carefully studied these things and have concluded, based on the evidence, that I can confidently trust the prophet." Rather, he said without elaboration, "I choose to believe the prophet," and the tone of his voice strongly implied an unspoken "and you'd better set aside your objections and believe him as well."

As I mentioned earlier, this strong appeal to unquestioned authority can sometimes be seen in Christian circles as well. An example that stands out in my mind is the experience of Fiona. She is a friend of Heidi's and mine from a summer we spent working with a church in London, England. She later got involved in a highly authoritarian church. When I saw her on a subsequent speaking trip to the UK, I could immediately see the negative effects on her normally vibrant and vivacious personality. Rather than being her usual joyful self whom we'd known years earlier, Fiona had become extremely cautious. She was nervous about something as simple as coming to say hello to me where I was teaching—simply because it was in a different church.

She did show up, but when I had the chance to sit down and talk with her, she anxiously admitted that she was fearful about being there. "I really should have gotten permission from my pastor or the church's elders to even be here," she told me. "Especially since I'm not sure that the things I'll hear today will completely line up with what my church teaches."

I replied, with a bit of intentional naiveté, "But surely these leaders would want you to think for yourself and learn to test ideas and become someone who can discern what it true and worth believing—right? Isn't that part of growing up spiritually?"

"Actually, I don't think they would agree with that, Mark," she replied hesitantly. "I guess I wish they were more like that—though I'm not criticizing them. Mostly I think they just want all of us in the church to submit to their teaching and authority so that we'll stay away from temptations and deluding influences, and keep becoming more like Jesus. It's like the Bible talks about—being good disciples of Christ and obeying the leaders he's put over his church."

I did my best to help her see that this was an unhealthy level of control and that the Bible does not teach us as Christians to practice that kind of blind obedience. I also tried to help her look in the mirror to see the negative impact this influence was having on her personality and even on her physical demeanor. But she wasn't ready at that point to question the teachings of these leaders or to acknowledge the ways it was hurting her as a person.

Thankfully, soon after that time I discovered a book called *The Subtle Power of Spiritual Abuse*[1] and was able to send Fiona a copy. I was afraid she wouldn't read it but would instead take it to her church the next Sunday and give it to the pastor. I imagined getting an irate phone call at some odd hour of the night from a fundamentalist minister with a strong English accent. But she didn't do that. I suppose because of the love and trust she felt in her friendship with Heidi and me, she actually did read the book. Doing so helped to embolden her over time to do what I would encourage you to do if you've embraced your faith primarily through a strong authority in your life. She tested the credibility of that authority and asked herself honest questions about the impact it was having on her life. For Fiona, this led to her eventually breaking away from that spiritually stifling situation. She didn't throw away her faith, but she learned to live it out in a healthier and, I believe, more God-honoring way. Today, she's part of a great church, and she's really glad she mustered the courage to make these changes in her life.

There's no doubt that blind or unquestioning reliance on authority can have negative effects on our lives—and not just in the area of faith.

Certainly in politics there are numerous examples of leaders who have had too much autonomy and abused their power to control not just small groups of people, but entire nations. One doesn't need to reflect long to think of names like Stalin, Hitler, and Mao Tse-tung—or more recently, Pol Pot, Saddam Hussein, and Kim Jong Il—and the devastation they wrought in the lives of untold numbers of people. While those names are well known, there are countless less-recognized leaders who wield unrestrained influence over many, in part because their authority is rarely challenged.

What about medical examples? I have a friend whose elderly mother, Helen, was experiencing excruciating pain in her back and shoulder. She kept getting increasingly ill until one day she started vomiting blood. Her family rushed her to her doctor, who gave her what seemed like a thorough examination. His diagnosis? Helen was having an allergic reaction to seasonal pollen, and she needed to take medications that would help her body deal with the allergens that were causing her so much soreness and discomfort. Relieved, the family took her back home, started her on the antihistamines and painkillers, and trusted that things would be better soon.

Well, things actually got worse. Eventually, they took Helen to the emergency room to find out if something more serious might be going on. She was admitted to the hospital, and they ran her through a gamut of tests. After a couple of days the results came back, and they pointed to a far different diagnosis: Helen wasn't struggling with allergies; she had cancer in her lungs, bones, lymph nodes, and liver. Four days later, she was dead. Needless to say, the original doctor was one authority who should have been questioned.

And what about authorities in educational institutions? How many theories have we been adamantly taught, especially in the area of science, that later were revised or completely refuted? (Or perhaps a better question might be this: How many theories are we *still* being taught that are right now in the process of being discredited?) The changes in prevailing paradigms are so regular and expected that one philosopher of science, Thomas Kuhn, wrote a fascinating book documenting this pattern. It's called *The Structure of Scientific Revolutions*.[2] Unfortunately, many times the academic authorities fail to present their "truths" in light of the reality that scientific theories come and go.

And as we've illustrated, both history and the daily news are filled with stories of religious authorities who overlook common sense and ignore known facts in order to teach their strange doctrines. In many cases they contradict the moral and ethical teachings they claim to represent. They discredit what they say by what they do. Yet through their charismatic personalities—and often political or financial clout—they gain control over the lives of the people "under" them. Increasingly, they wield their influence to gain support and subservience from their flock of faithful followers. Many of these "spiritual leaders" have wreaked havoc in the lives of their followers, not to mention creating confusion about God and matters of faith.

Harder to detect are the well-meaning teachers who try to live out their faith's tenets but who unwittingly communicate spiritual ideas that are not grounded in fact or history. The questionable authority is the religious system itself, with its collection of prophets, doctrines, and holy books. These situations demand a deeper digging into the history and foundations of the faith, because there may be serious flaws and faulty teachings at the very root of its structure. It was this kind of issue I was raising with the imam at the mosque; I didn't doubt his sincerity or commitment. I was questioning the actual foundations of his religion's claims.

At this point, you may think that I'm completely anti-authoritarian and would perhaps propose some sort of radical libertarianism to free us from all who would exercise influence over us. Far from it. I'm no anarchist, and I happen to think that John Mellencamp made a good point when he sang the line, "I fight authority; authority always wins."[3] The question is not *if* we'll be under authority, but *which* authorities we'll trust and respond to.

Can you imagine a world without any authorities to lead, teach, coach, or protect us? It would be one in which you'd have to become the expert on everything, and you'd have to fend for yourself and your loved ones in every arena. The phrase "every man for himself" would take on a new meaning. Images of the movie *Mad Max* come to mind.

In spite of the examples of power abuse, isn't it good we have those in government who exercise leadership in our lives—and who serve to protect us and to provide a civil environment in which we can do our work, raise our families, and live our lives? The Bible says that governments are a gift from God (a challenging idea to hold on to in some situations, I realize). Aren't you thankful for medical specialists who, as a general rule, help us preserve our health? And aren't you grateful for quality educators? I've certainly spent plenty of time and money in their schools, as you have, and have benefited from what I've learned. The list of important authorities in our lives could be expanded almost endlessly, including law enforcement officers, honest lawyers (no, that's not an oxymoron), health inspectors, border patrol agents, marriage counselors, automobile mechanics, tax accountants, real estate appraisers, and so on.

We trust these authorities because they have the education, expertise, and experience that add up to compelling credentials. For example, we don't trust just anyone claiming to be a doctor. We trust doctors with plaques up on their walls certifying that they went to—and graduated from—the right kinds of schools, gaining training and degrees that are relevant to the needs for which we go to them. The strength of our confidence in them is generally commensurate with the strength of their credentials.

Maybe you noticed in my earlier examples that it was actually other authorities in the same fields who brought awareness and correction to the abuses or errors. For instance, it was other doctors who finally diagnosed Helen's condition accurately. And it is those in the intellectual world of study and research who usually bring correctives to the various scientific and academic theories that need revision. So when the world is working the way it seems it should, it's usually better authorities—serving as checks and balances and offering "second opinions"—who are able to improve upon the deficiencies of the previous authorities.

The same is often true in the spiritual realm. The practical challenge for us, as it relates to the goal of finding a confident faith, is to muster up the courage and the clarity to reconsider and test the credentials of the spiritual authorities in our lives. These may be people or organizations that are already in leadership roles over us, or those that would like to be. We need to scrutinize what they say, do, and teach, and then compare and contrast them to other spiritual authorities, always looking to see whether they exhibit the marks of truthfulness and spiritual authenticity.

What are some of the specific criteria we can employ to put these authorities to the test? How can we apply the biblical wisdom of the apostle Paul when he warned us to "test everything. . . . Hold on to what is good. Stay away from every kind of evil"?[4]

Let me offer a few key characteristics to look for in order to establish whether an authority figure, an organization—or, for that matter, the religion's founder, writings, and coleaders—has the right kind of credentials. Though this is not an exhaustive list, I trust it will provide some practical guidance out of which you can examine and then confirm or deny the authorities affecting your life of faith.

INTEGRITY

This first characteristic might seem obvious, but it is often overlooked—especially after a person has been under someone's authority for a long time. The tendency is to let familiarity and trust grow to the point where inconsistencies or a lack of integrity are overlooked, and the leaders are treated as exceptions (and thus somehow above scrutiny) rather than as examples.

It's interesting to see what Jesus said about this in the Sermon on the Mount:

> Beware of false prophets who come disguised as harmless
> sheep but are really vicious wolves. You can identify
> them by their fruit, that is, by the way they act. Can
> you pick grapes from thornbushes, or figs from thistles?
> A good tree produces good fruit, and a bad tree
> produces bad fruit.[5]

We should be wary of leaders who talk a good game but who don't play by the rules themselves. If words about love, honesty, integrity, and humility are just that—mere words contradicted by actual actions—we'd be wise to look elsewhere for guidance in matters of faith. By the same token, impeccable integrity lends credence to a leader's words and teachings.

To make this point, Jesus actually taunted his critics and accusers, challenging them to point out even one flaw or inconsistency in his life. He said, "Which of you can truthfully accuse me of sin? And since I am telling you the truth, why don't you believe me?"[6] Obviously, this isn't a challenge you want to throw out to your attackers unless you've lived an astonishingly consistent life of integrity. But his critics and accusers were left speechless. Other than making up stories and false accusations, they had nothing to say.

Now, to be fair, it's possible that a leader is simply a poor representation of a worthy faith. But if these inconsistencies are rampant throughout the entire system, it's time to consider another place to grow in your faith.

CONSISTENCY

This is an extension of the last point—integrity—but applied over time. *Consistency* says that integrity must be lived out over the long haul. Any clever person can look good for a season—like the guy on a first or second date who can dress and act in civilized ways. But the grind of daily life tends to reveal a person's true character.

I'm not talking about an occasional lapse that may occur and cast a shadow on a person's typically good character. I'm talking about a fatal flaw that proves itself over time to be impervious to challenge or correction. Leaders can and do fail, but someone with integrity and consistency will get back up, humbly acknowledge his or her mistakes, make needed changes, implement safeguards and accountabilities, and move forward in greater fidelity toward what is good and right. King David is an example of this. He failed miserably, but he owned up to it, made important changes, and moved on. You can read his confession and sense his remorse in Psalm 51. It was his repentant attitude that led to further seasons of effective leadership in his life.

Just as it is wise in a courtship situation to look carefully and patiently at the other person to try to discern his or her real character, we should examine the life of the leader (or leaders) who represent our faith. This includes the founder as well as leaders currently at the helm. Try to look beneath the surface and do honest "gut checks" to see if you might discern subtle concerns. No one wants to end up following characters like Jim Jones or David Koresh, nor do we want to embrace a faith based on misguided leaders and ideas from decades or even centuries ago.

Also, it's important to ask God for wisdom along the way, even if you're dealing with doubts. A man once brought his son to Jesus for healing. When Jesus told him that "anything is possible if a person believes," the father instantly uttered these transparent words to Jesus: "I do believe, but help me overcome my unbelief!"[7] It was a vulnerable thing for the man to say, but Jesus didn't scold him for doubting. Instead, he answered the man's sincere request and healed his son.

So ask God for his help and guidance as you seek wisdom on these important matters of faith.

ACCURACY

Accuracy is critically important because it relates to the precision and authenticity of the leader's teachings. The apostle Paul gave an apt caution to his apprentice Timothy when he warned him, "Keep a close watch on how you live and on your teaching. Stay true to what is right."[8] We addressed the "how you live" part under "Integrity" and "Consistency"; now let's look at the "close watch on your teaching" part.

To put it concisely, a leader's teaching must be: (1) true to the world; (2) true to the leader's own words; and ultimately, (3) true to God's words.

True to the world means that what they say about verifiable areas in the physical realm needs to be accurate and true. If a so-called spiritual leader starts with the premise that the earth is flat, buyer beware. Jesus said it like this: "If you don't believe me when I tell you about earthly things, how can you possibly believe if I tell you about heavenly things?"[9]

For example, Mormon teachings (and thus, Mormon authority) suffer under this first test. Their writings and teachers make clear claims about entire civilizations that allegedly lived in the ancient Americas. The details about these peoples were purportedly written on golden tablets that were translated by Joseph Smith Jr. in the early 1800s. But you can't see or test the golden tablets because, according to the story, an angel "whisked them away" after Smith was done with them.

You also can't verify anything about these ancient civilizations because historians have discovered no evidence that they ever existed. Furthermore, the Smithsonian Institution sends out a form letter to anyone who inquires saying, "The

Book of Mormon is a religious document and not a scientific guide. The Smithsonian Institution has never used it in archaeological research, and any information that you have received to the contrary is incorrect."[10] In an earlier form of the same letter, which they sent out for years, titled "Statement Regarding the Book of Mormon," they forthrightly declared: "Smithsonian archaeologists see no direct connection between the archaeology of the New World and the subject matter of the book."[11]

And finally, a recent study showed conclusive DNA evidence that the Native American people on the North American continent share no genetic links with the Israelites or any other Middle Eastern people group, contradicting the clear claims in the Book of Mormon that these so-called Lamanites were of Hebrew descent. On the contrary, the DNA studies showed that these people were actually descended from Asian ancestors.[12]

I know these are hard facts for our Mormon friends to hear, but if their books and prophets can't be verified in regard to these "earthly things," it ought to give them strong pause about believing their books and prophets when they talk about unseen spiritual things. The principle of *accuracy* is one we all must be willing to apply as we test the teachings of would-be spiritual authorities in our own lives, including any writings that claim to be scriptural.

True to their own words means that the leaders must not only be honest and consistent, as we've said, but they must also prove to be right about things they declare to be true. For example, when a pastor with a healing ministry proclaims that a person "has been healed of polio," that person had better have had the symptoms in the first place and then be truly free of those symptoms tonight, tomorrow, and six months from now. Otherwise, the words—and the credibility—of that pastor prove empty.

When someone declares "in the name of the Lord" that a specific event is about to happen, yet that event fails to materialize, your trust in that "prophet" or alleged representative of God ought to fail to materialize as well. Look at these powerful words of warning from Moses in the Old Testament:

> *You may wonder, "How will we know whether or not*
> *a prophecy is from the LORD?" If the prophet speaks in*
> *the LORD's name but his prediction does not happen*
> *or come true, you will know that the LORD did not*
> *give that message. That prophet has spoken without my*
> *authority and need not be feared.*[13]

This is a warning worth heeding in regard to any message that claims to be prophetic. For example, if you have ever considered the teachings of the Jehovah's Witnesses, you should be aware that their "prophets" have made repeated false predictions about the return of Christ. According to their earliest teachers, the Battle of Armageddon and the destruction of all world powers would happen in 1914. When that didn't happen, they reinterpreted the prophecy and put out a new edition—it would all happen in 1918. Oops! Well, it would occur by 1925 for sure. This pattern of revising and updating went on repeatedly throughout the twentieth century, including more recent predictions for

1975.[14] Not only that, but one of their clearest and boldest prophecies, which was printed on the front of every *Alive* magazine until recent years, proclaimed that we would experience the fulfillment of "the Creator's promise of a peaceful and secure new world before the generation that saw the events of 1914 passes away." Needless to say, the clock has run out on that prophecy as well.

Before feeling fully settled with your faith, you owe it to yourself to make sure that the leaders of that faith system are true to their own words—especially when they claim to be speaking words from God on which you will stake your life.

True to God's words means that the doctrines being espoused must square with the teachings of God's revelation, the Bible. Though the Bible presents many teachings about many things, there is a relatively small set of core essentials that every trustworthy church leader will embrace and proclaim without reservation.

These include orthodox teachings about

- God (including the biblical doctrine of the Trinity—that there is one God who eternally exists in three persons: Father, Son, and Holy Spirit);

- humankind (that we were created good, but starting in the Garden of Eden we chose to go our own way and became sinful, thus we are living separated from God);

- Jesus (he is the second person of the Trinity, who, according to Philippians 2, let go of the perks of heaven, humbled himself, took the form of a human servant, and ultimately died to purchase our forgiveness); and

- salvation (Jesus' death on the cross paid for our sins; we must confess our sins and turn from them, receive his payment as our substitute, and make him our Savior and Lord).

Much more can be said (including the arguments and information that will be presented in the later section of the book labeled "Twenty Arrows of Truth"), but suffice it to say that any authority worth following will faithfully teach and defend these essential doctrines of the faith—with vigor. If you sense someone in leadership is trying to reinvent or renege on these biblical nonnegotiables, it's time to look for a new leader.

OPENNESS

One more test of authority will suffice for now. The leader or organization worth following will not resist scrutiny in the areas we just discussed: integrity, consistency, and accuracy. Openness is an important component of integrity. True integrity has nothing to hide. Likewise, openness is necessary for evaluating consistency. How can you really know whether a person's integrity goes all the way to the depths of who he or she is if the person isn't open about it? So trustworthy spiritual leaders shouldn't mind living their lives as open books.[15]

Earlier, we noted that Jesus invited his critics to examine his life and try to uncover any shortcomings. The apostle Paul reflected this same kind of openness by the way he lived out his values amid the people he taught and led: "You know of our concern for you from the way we lived when we were with you. . . . Keep putting into practice all you learned and received from me—everything you heard from me and saw me doing. Then the God of peace will be with you."[16]

It might go without saying, but the kind of openness and humility I'm talking about are often not exhibited by religious leaders and organizations. Many are secretive, covering up their mistakes and hiding blunders and sins of the past—as well as concealing their sketchy financial practices in the present. They might put on a positive exterior, but when you start to ask too many questions or probe too deeply, that surface-level sweetness can quickly disappear as their defenses go up. Some even become hostile and threaten challengers with litigation or physical harm.

Whether their resistance is overt or a more benign neglect of your questions and your desire to test their authority, if you find a persistent lack of openness, red flags should go up in your mind. You should proceed with extreme caution, if at all. Authorities worth following—competent and confident ones—are not afraid of questions, and they don't have to apply intimidation or power to gain a following.

As you examine the spiritual authorities in your life and put them to the test using the criteria listed above, I believe it will help you move toward finding a worthwhile and trustworthy faith—one with credentials you can have confidence in.

My friend Nabeel was raised in an Islamic family whose members were among the most dedicated Muslims he had ever known. Although born a US citizen, he was taught to read the Qur'an in Arabic by the age of four, and he had read the entire book—and even memorized whole chapters of it—by the time he was five. As a young boy he was often held up as a model for other children in the local Islamic community. Growing up he continued studying the Qur'an as well as offering prayers five times a day and living for Allah in the most devoted way he knew how. Islam was not just his religion; it was his blueprint for life.

Then, in college, he became friends with a guy named David, who turned out to be a committed Christian. When Nabeel saw David reading his Bible one evening, he immediately challenged him, insisting that no reasonable person could trust the Christian Scriptures. This led to a series of impassioned discussions that spanned the next several years. They talked about some of the same issues I had raised with the imam in the mosque several years earlier: Did Jesus really claim to be the Son of God, was he crucified on a cross, and (probably the most important question) did he really rise from the dead?

Much to Nabeel's surprise, David offered strong logic and evidence for his beliefs. In fact, the deeper Nabeel looked and the harder he studied, the more he became convinced that David's answers made sense. This shook his confidence in the authority of the Muslim faith, so he asked Allah—repeatedly—to give him reassurance through answers to specific prayers and by speaking to him through dreams or visions. Those prayers were answered in uncanny ways—but not in the ways he had expected. Rather, they pointed him again and again to the truths David was presenting and away from the teachings of Islam.

Frustrated and desperate, Nabeel decided to put what he was discovering to the test by consulting with experts who might help him. He traveled to Washington, DC, to Canada, and to England in search of knowledgeable Muslims who might answer David's arguments against Islam. In the process, he heard a variety of responses which, as he describes it, "ran the gamut from terribly unconvincing to fairly innovative," and he encountered people who "ranged from sincere to condescendingly caustic." At the end of his research, the arguments for and against Islam still hung in the balance, but one thing had become abundantly clear in his mind: the information supporting Islam was far from approaching the strength of the case for Christianity.

Finally, after years of searching, Nabeel realized he needed to turn away from the spiritual authority that had been over his life since childhood and begin following a new one. That new authority was Jesus, who, Nabeel had finally come to believe, really was the Son of God who had died and risen to become the Savior of the world.

I deeply admire Nabeel for his courage to seek the truth and follow the evidence wherever it would lead, even when his journey became uncomfortable. More than that, I see in him someone who has done the diligent work of testing and refining his beliefs to make sure they are rooted in a firm foundation of truth. As a result, he's now one of the most confident Christians I know.[17]

Nabeel chose to step away from the Authoritarian faith path and primarily onto the Evidential faith path. I encourage you to take a good look at that path too. You can learn more about it in chapter 8. That path will lead you to examine the evidence for the Christian belief—and show you the way to a confident faith.

Here are some encouraging words from Nabeel to fellow travelers, about searching to make certain you're following the true God:

> *I invite you to search for Him and lay your current life on the line as I did. He is there, and He is waiting for you to come to Him so that He can walk with you. Since my conversion, God has filled me completely and guided me in His ways. He changed my life, and I invite you to let Him change your life. But be sure that you really are ready for your life to change; I guarantee you, it will. So it is written: you will be given a new self, created to be like God in true righteousness and holiness (Ephesians 4:24). My prayers are with you.*[18]

CHAPTER SIX

THE INTUITIVE FAITH PATH:
"Truth Is What You Feel in Your Heart"

It was a classic *Star Wars* moment.

Obi-Wan Kenobi, the Jedi Master, was training Luke Skywalker, his young apprentice, on how to effectively use his lightsaber in battle. But after a few failed attempts by Luke to hit a small, rapidly flying "seeker" remote, Obi-Wan decided it was time to instill some new insights into his student.

"I suggest you try it again, Luke," he said, as he placed a large helmet over Luke's head, including a blast shield that completely covered his eyes. "This time, let go of your conscious self and act on instinct. . . . Your eyes can deceive you. Don't trust them."

Obi-Wan then threw the remote into the air. It dropped straight down, and as Luke swung at it blindly and missed it yet again, it fired out a laser that hit Luke right in the seat of his pants. Luke let out a yelp as he swung wildly once more, trying in vain to hit it with his lightsaber.

"Stretch out with your feelings," Obi-Wan advised him.

Doing his best to apply the lesson, Luke stood in one place, seemingly frozen. The remote made another dive at him, and this time—surprisingly—he managed to deflect the laser.

"You see, you can do it," Obi-Wan encouraged.

"You know," Luke said to Obi-Wan, "I did feel something. I could almost see the remote."

"That's good," Obi-Wan replied. "You have taken your first step into a larger world."[1]

This scene from *Star Wars: A New Hope* offers a pretty good picture of what I'll refer to as the *Intuitive* faith path. People who take this path tend not to trust in their intellect or what their eyes and ears tell them, but rather in an inner sense—a spiritual instinct that they believe points them toward right ideas and actions.

If you've become a Christian primarily through the Intuitive path, you may feel quite confident about your faith—but you may not sense that same confidence in others when you tell them that you believe because you just know in your heart it's true. (The same applies to whatever belief system you've accepted.) Can a person find a firm foundation for a sure faith based on the intuitive insights they feel inside?

It's hard to argue with the fact that we truly are, as the Bible puts it, "fearfully and wonderfully made."[2] As amazingly complex *Homo sapiens*, we should not be surprised that God built into us some measure of intuitive instinct that works with our other senses—and perhaps sometimes even independently—to give us quick and clear impressions of dangers, opportunities, or direction. We know many animals have these instincts in various forms, so why not we humans, too?

In fact, we often talk in terms of instinct. It's widely accepted, for example, that women tend to have higher levels of extrasensory insight. We call it "woman's intuition."

Anyone who knows Heidi would realize that she dwarfs me with her sense of intuition. I tend to be more of a "knowledge person," who studies facts and information, often taking things at face value. "He seems like an honest guy," I'll tell Heidi, "and the product seems like a good one. I think we should buy from him." To which she replies, "I can see why you'd say that" (translation: *People like you, who lack the requisite radar, tend to fall for things like this*). "But I sense that something's not right about this guy and what he's telling us. I think we should look around some more before we make any purchases." I've been married to Heidi long enough, and have been tutored by past experience often enough, to have learned that I neglect her discernment only at great risk. She pretty much always turns out to be right.

On a broader level, we also know that certain people, male and female, have a more developed sense of awareness and insight, being able to read a room, an audience, or an individual—sometimes even from great distances. For example, they do it just by hearing a person's voice on the phone or by looking at someone's handwriting.

In the church, as well, we acknowledge that certain members of a congregation have unusual wisdom or discernment. Those who have these "spiritual gifts" are attuned to what is happening at deeper levels than normal observation would reveal. Whether this awareness is the person's routine way of functioning or only comes in occasional flashes of insight, it can be very helpful to the church's leaders in making decisions or avoiding danger.

Reliance on an inner sense is also a high value for people whose beliefs are influenced by Eastern religions in which the physical world and sensory experience are viewed as maya, or illusion, and truth is seen not as logical but as intuitive. "Stretch out with your feelings," Obi-Wan coached Luke. It was an approach based on the Buddhist-oriented philosophy of George Lucas, the writer and creative genius behind *Star Wars*.

In a *Time* interview with Bill Moyers, Lucas talked about the importance of taking a leap of faith: "You'll notice Luke uses that quite a bit through the film—not to rely on pure logic, not to rely on the computers, but to rely on faith. That is what that 'Use the Force' is: a leap of faith. There are mysteries and powers larger than we are, and you have to trust your feelings in order to access them."[3]

According to this approach, real perception resides in feelings and instinct. That's where people on the Intuitive path believe they'll find the most reliable sense of direction, though, it is claimed, it will often be gained in hidden places and be easily overlooked by the masses of people—who are caught up in the world of sights and sounds, and who are missing the deeper, esoteric realities only available to those who search them out using their innate sixth sense.

That's why Transcendental Meditation (TM) practitioners instruct their inductees to relax their minds, empty themselves of all conscious thought, and open up to what their teachers promise will be an internal sense of peace and wholeness (along with, many would argue, a whole raft of Hindu ideas). The founder of the Transcendental Meditation methodology, Maharishi Mahesh Yogi, said this during a talk he gave in Switzerland:

> With Transcendental Meditation, the activity of the mind settles down, and when the activity of the mind settles down, the mind is in the character of unbounded awareness. . . . It's like a wave in the ocean . . . settling down . . . unbounded quiet level of the water. So Transcendental Meditation creates this transcendental consciousness.[4]

Another philosopher who taught along these same lines was Dr. J. Krishnamurti of Oxford, England, who "located the human problem in our thoughts, a result of conditioning received during our lives as humans as we passed through various stages of intellectual development. He advocated 'freedom from thoughts' as the means of liberation."[5]

These views are not limited to the world of movies or Eastern meditation. Many New Age–oriented success teachers will coach you to stop trying to reason your way through life and to instead let your inner voice guide you in the ways you should go.

Napoleon Hill's 1937 classic, *Think and Grow Rich*, has been called the granddaddy of all motivational literature and has sold more than 30 million copies worldwide. Hill's ideas have influenced generations of business leaders and success seekers, as well as an entire industry of self-help books. In light of that sweeping impact, it's interesting to get his take on the subject of learning and deciding what to believe:

> *Throughout history, people have depended too much upon their physical senses and have limited their knowledge to physical things they could see, touch, weigh, and measure. We are now entering the most marvelous of all ages—an age which will teach us something of the intangible forces of the world about us. Perhaps we shall learn as we pass through this age, that the "other self" is more powerful than the physical self we see when we look in a mirror.*[6]

In a later chapter, "The Sixth Sense: The Door to the Temple of Wisdom," Hill adds these thoughts:

> *Somewhere in the cell structure of the human brain is an area which receives vibrations of thought ordinarily*

called hunches. So far, science has not discovered where this site of the sixth sense is located, but this is not important. The fact remains that human beings do receive accurate knowledge, through sources other than the five physical senses. . . .

Nearly all great leaders, such as Napoleon, Bismarck, Joan of Arc, Christ, Buddha, Confucius, and Muhammad, understood and made use of the sixth sense almost continuously. The major portion of their greatness consisted of their knowledge of this principle.

The sixth sense is not something that one can take off and put on at will. Ability to use this great power comes slowly.[7]

This emphasis on intuitive knowledge has been around for a long time, but it is growing in popularity and appeal, in part because of people like Napoleon Hill and others who have been similarly influential. But there is also an inherent intrigue factor at play. The idea of knowing things that others don't know, through internal, hidden processes, has a certain mystique and appeal. It also seems to sidestep the need for rigorous thought and study—or even accountability—opting instead for more direct forms of enlightenment.

The promise is also made that if you properly apply and focus your mental energy, it will bring great rewards. A more recent bestselling book is *The Secret*, by Rhonda Byrne, which expands on many of these ideas. Here's what Byrne says about the Intuitive approach, echoing some of Napoleon Hill's thoughts and mixing in a bit more of the mystical as well:

Trust your instincts. It's the Universe inspiring you. It's the Universe communicating with you on the receiving frequency. If you have an intuitive or instinctive feeling, follow it, and you will find that the Universe is magnetically moving you to receive what you asked for. . . .

Remember that you are a magnet, attracting everything to you. When you have gotten clear in your mind about what you want, you have become a magnet to draw those things to you, and those things you want are magnetized to you in return. The more you practice and begin to see the law of attraction bringing things to you, the greater the magnet you will become, because you will add the power of faith, belief, and knowing.[8]

Even in leadership circles and popular business books, it sometimes sounds as if intuition is winning out over information as the way to make the quickest and most reliable decisions. That's how some people interpret the popular book *Blink: The Power of Thinking without Thinking,* by bestselling author Malcolm Gladwell. In the opening pages, Gladwell tells the story of "The Statue That Didn't Look Right":

In September of 1983, an art dealer by the name of Gianfranco Becchina approached the J. Paul Getty Museum in California. He had in his possession, he said, a marble statue dating from the sixth century BC. It was what is known as a kouros—a sculpture of

a nude male youth standing with his left leg forward
and his arms at his sides. There are only about two
hundred kouroi in existence, and most have been
recovered badly damaged or in fragments from grave
sites or archeological digs. But this one was almost
perfectly preserved. It stood close to seven feet tall.
It had a kind of light-colored glow that set it apart
from other ancient works. It was an extraordinary
find. Becchina's asking price was just under
$10 million.[9]

The people at the Getty proceeded carefully. They took the Greek statue on loan, and then they went to work studying it and all of the documentation that came with it in order to determine if it was authentic. They analyzed core samples of the artifact using an electron microscope, electron microprobe, mass spectrometry, X-ray diffraction, and X-ray fluorescence, and they studied the layer of calcite on the surface of the statue, which appeared to be hundreds or even thousands of years old.[10]

After more than a year of critically examining this statue in every way they could dream up, they were finally satisfied and decided to make the grand purchase. In 1986, they put the celebrated sculpture on public display. This created so much excitement that the story made the front page of the *New York Times.*

But something wasn't right. As top art experts and historians saw the kouros in person, they candidly commented on how it just didn't look the way it should. It was hard for them to put a finger on the exact issue, but they sensed there was a problem. One world-class authority on Greek sculpture knew immediately upon seeing it that something was wrong. She just had "a hunch, an instinctive sense that something was amiss."[11]

When Thomas Hoving, former director of the Metropolitan Museum of Art, saw the statue, the first word that came to his mind was *fresh*. "And 'fresh,'" he said, "was not the right reaction to have to a two-thousand-year-old statue. . . . The kouros looked like it had been dipped in the very best caffè latte from Starbucks."[12] He told the museum curator that the Getty should not buy it; or if they already had, that they should try to get their money back. Another expert, this one from Greece, saw the statue and "immediately felt cold." He quickly determined that the work was a fake, because when he first laid his eyes on it, he felt a wave of what he described as "intuitive repulsion."[13]

Gladwell sums up the situation: "The Getty, with its lawyers and scientists and months of painstaking investigation, had come to one conclusion, and some of the world's foremost experts in Greek sculpture—just by looking at the statue and sensing their own 'intuitive repulsion'—had come to another. Who was right?"[14]

I'll bet you have a hunch about who was right. It turned out that the sculpture was in fact a forgery, and the intuitive experts had been vindicated. "In the first two seconds of looking—in a single glance—they were able to understand more about the essence of the statue than the team at the Getty was able to understand after fourteen months."[15]

I have a friend who called his travel agent to book a cross-country business trip. She advised him on the best flight to take to get to his destination, and upon gaining his approval, was in the process of typing in his reservation. As he heard her keying in the information, he suddenly felt that he ought to ask her on what airline she was booking him. As soon as she told him which carrier it was, he surprised her—and probably himself, too—when he blurted out, "I don't feel comfortable with that. What are my other options?"

She studied her computer screen for a moment and then said with some hesitation, "Well, you could fly a different airline into another nearby city, but it would be a significant distance from where you're trying to go. You'd have to rent a car and drive a lot farther. I'm sure you wouldn't want to do that . . ."

He again responded in an unexpected way: "Yes, that's what I'd like to do. Go ahead and book me into that other city." She complied with his request and booked him on the alternative flight, though she was probably shaking her head at his insistence on going so far out of his way.

A few weeks later, my friend boarded his airplane, which took off within ten minutes of the more convenient flight he had opted not to take. About ninety minutes later, he landed safely, had dinner at a restaurant near the airport, and got into his rental car for the long drive to his destination. That's when he turned on the radio—and heard the shocking news that the other flight had flipped over in the air and crashed as it was nearing the airport, killing everyone on board.

How did my friend know that he needed to switch flights? That's a great question, but the truth is he really didn't *know*. If you asked him why he made that abrupt decision on the phone with the travel agent, he wouldn't tell you he heard a voice from heaven or even a subtle spiritual whisper. He simply felt that he needed to go on the other flight. He trusted his instinct and is alive today to talk about it.

It's worth adding that we all have an inward moral intuition, or what we call our conscience, that guides us concerning right and wrong. This ethical compass gives us a sense of direction about standards we should live by—but we would generally understand it to be a natural phenomenon (though God-given), not a special revelation from God.

It is interesting, too, that spiritual leaders in biblical times sometimes made decisions based on an intuitive sense. The apostle Paul, for example, after arriving at a certain town where he wanted to minister, said, "I had no peace of mind because my dear brother Titus hadn't yet arrived with a report from you. So I said good-bye and went on to Macedonia to find him."[16] There was no divine voice, no angelic guidance, no prophetic word—just a guy who lacked peace, followed his feelings, and made what seemed to be a wise decision.

In light of the avalanche of examples of the power of intuition, why not just go with it? Why not feel our way through our daily decisions, including deciding what to believe in the spiritual realm?

That was the approach of a woman who worked at a gift shop in La Jolla, California. When Heidi made a casual comment to her about a spiritual theme, this lady was quick to speak up about her strong faith. As we talked with her, we discovered it was a faith in a variety of New Age ideas, including the power of horoscopes and the insights of fortune-tellers. Her deeply held beliefs also included a "Jesus" who she said was very close to her, who would never tell anyone they were wrong or judge them for their actions, and who seemed to be completely aligned with her own views on all these things. When I tried to raise the issue of what Jesus actually taught about some of these topics, she bristled. "My Jesus isn't like that," she said emphatically. She knew this—because she could feel it in her heart.

If God is wise, powerful, and full of knowledge, then it certainly follows that he is able to give us data that goes beyond the normal information available through our senses. We may not even know where it emanates from, but it can help us in very important ways.

So we see that we are endowed with instincts and insights that can make enormous differences in our lives. Blaise Pascal said famously, *"Le coeur a ses raisons que la raison ne connaît point,"* which translates, "The heart has its reasons of which reason knows nothing."[17] When we need to size up a person or a situation, we're wise to consult our hearts—or, as it's put in business circles, we should "do a gut check." This can save us a lot of heartache along the way.

But we need to be careful, too. Many hearts have been broken—and lives shattered—by following the heart alone. Hunches, intuitive flashes, and "gut feelings" can serve as cautionary alerts—but whenever possible, these need to be tested against other proven methods for finding or scrutinizing truth. In other words, they can be great warning lights, but in isolation they're generally not navigation systems to give us detailed directions in our daily decisions.

To illustrate the limited nature of intuitive information, let's look back through some of the examples we've discussed, starting with the scene from *Star Wars*. Do you remember that Obi-Wan Kenobi put the helmet on Luke Skywalker and told him to stop using his eyes and to just act on instinct? But notice that Obi-Wan failed to heed his own advice. That is, he didn't proceed to put a helmet over his own head and block his own sight in order to more instinctively sense how Luke was doing. Instead, he stood and observed him the old-fashioned way—with his two eyes—which were just like the ones he had told Luke not to be deceived by. So much for "stretching out with your feelings."

And what are we to make of the advice of the Transcendental Meditation teachers who say we need to empty our minds and think about nothing? First, we have to wonder if it's even possible. I mean, how would we *know* that we were actually thinking about nothing without harboring in our minds the thought, *I'm finally thinking about nothing*? In that case we'd actually be *thinking about* thinking about nothing, which is a thought in and of itself—one that would disqualify us at that very moment from thinking about nothing.

I also agree with this incisive critique:

> *The guru who tells us that our thoughts are the problem*
> *has reached this conclusion and communicates it to us*
> *only by use of the very faculties that he decries. We are*

caught in a web of contradiction from which there is no
escape. In fact, the logical conclusion of this philosophy
is total silence—absence of communication. An ancient
Indian scripture called the Kenopanishad has this
unaffirmable quote: "He who speaks does not know,
and he who knows does not speak."[18]

In many ways, this approach shows itself to be self-contradictory and self-defeating and therefore eliminates itself as being a viable option.

And what of Napoleon Hill and his bold assertion that we were entering the age of hunches and reliance on our sixth sense? It's interesting that his conclusions throughout *Think and Grow Rich* were drawn from a lifetime of study and observation. In fact, the title page of the book affirms that it was "organized through 25 years of research, in collaboration with more than 500 distinguished men of great wealth, who proved by their achievements that this philosophy is practical." In other words, Hill didn't get the bulk of his information from instinct, hunches, or sixth-sense insights. He got it the old-fashioned way, by rigorous research and careful observation, and then he logically laid out what he'd discovered. He was perhaps aided by intuition and instinct (and also, it could be argued, a fair amount of speculation), but it certainly was not in isolation from these other, more normal approaches to learning.

And think back to the story of the Greek statue. Who were those men and women who had the correct initial "blink" reactions? They weren't just intuitive people pulled off the street. No, they were specialists in the study of ancient sculptures and artifacts. In other words, they were knowledgeable men and women with well-trained instincts. Their hunches were *informed* hunches, and these were supported by their awareness of broader evidence and information. And even after these world-class experts experienced "intuitive repulsions" and communicated their concerns about the statue, the Getty people still did further research—of the traditional, scientific kind—to test and verify the warnings they'd received.

Malcolm Gladwell recognizes the limitations of intuition and even offers a caveat in the introduction to his book: "*Blink* is not just a celebration of the power of the glance, however. I'm also interested in those moments when our instincts betray us. . . . When should we trust our instincts, and when should we be wary of them? . . . When our powers of rapid cognition go awry, they go awry for a very specific and consistent set of reasons, and those reasons can be identified and understood. . . . The third and most important task of this book is to convince you that our snap judgments and first impressions can be educated and controlled."[19] Gladwell spends the latter part of the book qualifying the use of initial impressions and teaching readers how to train, inform, and guide their intuitive sense.

And the feeling my friend had that he needed to book the other flight? Well, he told me later that he was aware at the time that the airline he was almost booked on had struggled with safety issues in recent years. So that knowledge was likely influencing him, even if not overtly. It's also possible, and I think very likely, that there was some unseen divine intervention protecting and guiding him, though below the level of consciousness. There's no need to conclude that this was merely an unguided intuitive sixth sense. Rather, it was likely a confluence of his own thoughts based on relevant data and information, along with instincts and perhaps supernatural protection.

What about psychics and others who claim to have special access to the mysteries of truth and knowledge? If they really had the intuitive insights they claim to have, do you think they'd be sitting around in shoddy little booths reading sweaty palms for paltry sums of money? No, they'd be rich from playing the lottery and the stock market, because they'd know exactly when to buy their tickets and where to lay down their investments. Their lack of success betrays their lack of insight.

It's worth noting that, generally speaking, even the most ardent promoters of the Intuitive approach ignore that approach when it comes to everyday living. That's why they drive down the highway with their eyes wide open (not wearing helmets with blast shields covering their faces, thankfully), check the expiration dates on food before they buy it, study the financial health of businesses before they invest in them, and get advanced degrees in areas that are important to their careers—none of which seems to model the purported priority of intuitive knowledge.

It's also interesting that those who advocate the intuitive way of knowing routinely write detailed logical defenses of it, trying to support it with evidence and examples drawn from daily life. They don't tell you just to clutch their books to your heart or hold them over your head as you decide through some sixth sense if what they are saying is true. Rather, they give you *reasons* to trust them, to buy their books, and to listen to their lectures—reasons that at least to some degree undermine the main thrust of their approach.

What then should we conclude about intuition? It is, at best, an imperfect guide—one that needs to be tested and affirmed by other means. It's like a flashing yellow light near a dark intersection on a stormy night. We should pay attention to it, but also slow down, look both ways, and seek further information. Intuition can be very helpful, but it rarely tells us all we need to know. In addition, it can be misleading. We tend to forget all the times our intuition was wrong and selectively remember the times—even if rare—when it was actually right.

I should add that the writers of the Bible caution us to be suspicious of our own independent assessments. Solomon, for example, the wisest man who ever lived, warned ominously in the book of Proverbs, "There is a path before each person that seems right, but it ends in death."[20] Add to that the writings of the prophet Jeremiah: "The human heart is the most deceitful of all things, and desperately wicked."[21] That's a strong indictment, but if you look through the window of history or into the mirror of your own life, it's also hard to refute.

If you want to be confident in your faith, then pay attention to your instincts, but also remember you must scrutinize and corroborate them carefully. You need to test what you intuit against logic and evidence. For more about how to do that, read chapter 8, which describes the Evidential faith path. Also, you should honestly assess what you think in light of Jesus' actual teachings. Don't let Napoleon Hill, a New Age book, or your inner voice tell you what Jesus meant to convey. Don't go by what you imagine or wish he had said. Instead, look at what he actually *did* say in the four Gospels of the New Testament: Matthew, Mark, Luke, and John.

In other words, *let Jesus speak for himself.* He's the one who declared, "My sheep listen to my voice; I know them, and they follow me."[22]

CHAPTER SEVEN

THE MYSTICAL FAITH PATH:
"Truth Is What You Think God Told You"

"I've read the Book of Mormon, and I prayed and asked the Heavenly Father to show me if it was true—as it tells us to do in Moroni chapter 10—and God clearly answered my prayers," a sweet teenager named Rachael said earnestly to me and others sitting around the table.[1]

"I can tell you with all my heart that I know this book is true," she continued, her voice trembling and tears welling up in her eyes as she clutched the Mormon scriptures. "And if you'll just pray and ask the Father the way I did, he'll show you the same thing he showed me. This book is so precious to me, and I love God so much—I just want everybody to know this too. . . ." Her voice trailed off as she was overwhelmed with emotion.

It was a tender moment, though an admittedly awkward

one. No one could doubt Rachael's sincerity, nor did anyone want to venture a differing opinion, out of respect for her and the heartfelt testimony she'd just given.

If you've identified the *Mystical* faith path as the primary path that has led you to your convictions, stories like Rachael's may make you a little uncomfortable. If you've received what you're confident is God's inner peace and assurance about your faith, and someone else claims to have received a similar kind of peace and assurance about their contradictory beliefs, then how can you know whose assurance is real?

Let's face it: claims of mystical encounters with supernatural beings—whether spirits, angels, departed loved ones, or even God the Father himself—are hard to argue with. Frankly, they are difficult, if not impossible, to disprove (or prove). Even if you're not convinced that the implications of the testimony are true, it's natural to think, *Who am I to tell this girl that the Book of Mormon is fraught with inconsistencies, or that her church has a long record of unsupported speculation and stories?* And it's equally natural to wonder, *If she can have a religious experience that I'm convinced isn't real, then how can I be sure that my religious experience is real?*

So how can we deal with these kinds of claims? Let's back up and examine this approach to establishing one's beliefs, which I'm calling the Mystical faith path. This one goes beyond the Intuitive method we discussed in chapter 6, because it entails not just a human instinct or some kind of natural "sixth sense" that leads a person to certain conclusions. Rather, the Mystical method bases its position on claims of an actual encounter with a supernatural entity. And because this path tends to be more spiritual in nature, you'll see that some of the ways we need to test it are also of a more spiritual nature.

Here's an initial observation: not all mystical claims are created equal. For example, consider the man I met years ago in Orange County, California, who confided to me that he was one of the two prophets described in the last book of the Bible and predicted to appear sometime near the end of the world.[2] I wondered what I had done to be worthy of such an astounding disclosure—and was surprised that a person of such importance would be hanging out in a shabby sandwich shop in downtown Santa Ana.

That experience was strange, but not quite as odd as my encounter with a man to whom I gave a ride from a music festival. (I know you're not supposed to pick up hitchhikers, but he knew some of my friends and seemed normal enough—at first.) Things started getting weird about midway through our journey from Madison to Chicago. I don't know whether he viewed me as trustworthy, gullible, or both, but he decided to let me in on an astonishing secret: *he was the Holy Spirit!*

Well, to be fair, he actually claimed that his title was "The Comforter," based on Jesus' description of the Holy Spirit in John 16. Needless to say, I was a bit taken aback, especially when he went on to explain that he had been present during the events described in the first chapter of Genesis— and had, in fact, participated in the creation of the world. Now, I've never claimed to grasp all of the intricacies of the

Christian doctrine of the Trinity, but I was pretty sure that "The Comforter" sitting in the passenger seat of my Nissan wasn't a member of it.

Or there was the time when I was helping an elderly couple in the stereo store where I worked, and the woman decided to broach a spiritual discussion. When she saw I was open to talking about the subject, she decided to venture a step further. "God did a wonderful miracle in my husband's life many years ago," she said. "Can we tell you about it?"

"Sure," I said, always interested in such things. With that, her husband, who had been silent up until that point, could not contain his pent-up enthusiasm. "A number of years ago, I died," he exclaimed in excited tones. "And God worked through a wonderful prophet, who prayed over my body and raised me back to life again."

"Really?" I asked, sensing the sincerity of their claim while trying to hide my incredulity. "That's amazing."

Maybe you've encountered these kinds of stories in your own life. Perhaps a friend has passed along a similar account, or you've seen fantastic claims on the Internet. They tell you about someone they know (actually, it's more often a friend of a friend—or was it the friend's uncle?) who had an amazing experience. A man these people had given a ride warned them about the imminent end of the world, and then—*poof*—he disappeared. They can't remember the guy's name or the date it actually happened, but one thing's for sure: *it was an angel in the backseat.*

What are we to make of these things? How can we sort out the real facts, if there are any, from fiction? It may not seem very important when it comes to rumors of angels riding in who-knows-whose car on the back roads of Arkansas in the early 1970s, or of supposedly earthshaking events like scientists discovering hell in Siberia (did you hear about that one?). But when people like you or me or Rachael start basing our beliefs on mystical encounters, it becomes supremely important.

Let me introduce the first of two important guidelines to help us evaluate mystical encounters:

FEEL ≠ REAL

I have no question that Rachael felt something when she prayed over her copy of the Book of Mormon. I'm far less confident about the end-times prophet in Santa Ana, the Comforter/Creator guy in my car, or the man claiming to have been raised from the dead—though it's possible each was sincere in thinking he had experienced something out of the ordinary. But what they *feel* does not necessarily equate with something that's *real*.

Let's look more deeply at Rachael's claim, which was touching in its presentation but predictable in its content. I've heard many Mormons give this same testimony over the years. Though it may reflect a sensation they actually felt, it's also part of their religious culture, their training, and the expectation among their members—and it is central to their evangelistic appeal.

One of the chief defenders of Mormonism today is Robert L. Millet, professor of ancient scripture and former dean of religious education at Brigham Young University. He wrote a book called *Getting at the Truth: Responding to Difficult Questions about LDS Beliefs*, which apparently is designed to be a training manual for members of the Mormon religion (officially called the Church of Jesus Christ of Latter-Day Saints—thus the "LDS" in the book title).

What follows are some examples of what Millet says about how to sort out one's beliefs, including several quotes from high-level Mormon leaders. Read these words carefully; they provide a great example of the Mystical approach:

> *The most tried and true method of obtaining divine direction—[is] prayer itself.*[3]

> *In a very real sense,* believing is seeing. *No member of the Church need feel embarrassed at being unable to produce the golden plates or the complete Egyptian papyrus. No member of the Church should hesitate to bear testimony of verities that remain in the realm of faith, that are* seen only with the eyes of faith.[4]

> *President Ezra Taft Benson pointed out:* "We do not have to prove the Book of Mormon is true. The book is its own proof. All we need to do is read it and declare it. . . . *We are not required to prove that the Book of Mormon is true or is an authentic record through external evidences—though there are many. It never has been the case, nor is it so now, that the*

studies of the learned will prove the Book of Mormon true or false. The origin, preparation, translation, and verification of the truth of the Book of Mormon have all been retained in the hands of the Lord, and the Lord makes no mistakes. You can be assured of that."[5]

President Gordon B. Hinckley put things in proper perspective when he taught [regarding the Book of Mormon], . . . "The evidence for its truth, for its validity in a world that is prone to demand evidence, lies not in archaeology or anthropology, though these may be helpful to some. It lies not in word research or historical analysis, though these may be confirmatory. The evidence for its truth and validity lies within the covers of the book itself. The test of its truth lies in reading it. *It is a book of God. Reasonable individuals may sincerely question its origin, but* those who read it prayerfully may come to know by a power beyond their natural senses that it is true."[6]

Notice how this method of "knowing" truth is then turned into an approach for "showing" it to others:

Elder Boyd K. Packer declared, . . . "Do not be ill at ease or uncomfortable because you can give little more than your conviction. . . . If we can stand without shame, without hesitancy, without embarrassment, without reservation to bear witness that the gospel has been restored, that there are prophets and Apostles upon the earth, that the truth is available for all mankind,

*the Lord's Spirit will be with us. And that assurance
can be affirmed to others."*[7]

In the end, the only way that the things of God can
be known is by the power of the Holy Ghost. . . .
The only way spiritual truths may be known is by
the quiet whisperings of the Holy Ghost.[8]

Then, near the close of this discussion, Millet attempts to
assure his readers by giving his own testimony:

*I am grateful to have, burning within my soul,
a testimony that the Father and the Son appeared
to Joseph Smith in the Spring of 1820, and that the
Church of Jesus Christ of Latter-Day Saints is truly
the kingdom of God on earth.*[9]

So built on this experiential, mystical foundation, the
strategy of the Mormon missionaries at your door is to give
some introductory information about their founder and
prophet, Joseph Smith Jr., his stories of early visions (yes,
he built his beliefs on the Mystical approach, too), and their
claims concerning the origins of the Book of Mormon. Next,
they'll testify to you about their own experiences of having
been assured by God that it's all true. Then they'll get to
their real bottom line, which is to challenge you to do what
they've done: take the Book of Mormon, read a portion of
it, and then get on your knees and ask the Heavenly Father
to show you if it's true.

The approach is simple, and it has proven very effective—

Mormonism has long been one of the faster-growing religious movements in the United States. So what, if anything, is wrong with the method?

Well, for one thing, it is built on the assumption that *feel* must equal *real*. Specifically, if you pray the way they asked you to, and you feel anything remotely resembling a "burning in your soul," then you're supposed to accept that everything they told you is true, and it's time to become a Mormon.

But let me venture some other reasons a person might feel something.

First, many who accept this challenge to sit down, read the Book of Mormon, and pray to God—alone, unforced, and unrelated to any church services or holiday meals with the family—are folks who haven't done these kinds of things in years, if ever. So they're already feeling more spiritual than usual, just because they're reading a faith-oriented book and doing a religious-oriented activity. *There must be a God,* they think, *to get someone like me to take this stuff seriously.*

When they finally get on their knees to pray, they naturally feel warm feelings—due to the simple fact that they are bowing before their Maker. This is the most saintly thing they've done in years! At this point, it is easy to see how these positive emotions could be misinterpreted to mean that the entire Mormon story is actually *true*.

Second, as they read the Book of Mormon some of it sounds familiar and seems to have a distinctive ring of truth. Why is that? It might be because whole sections were copied almost word-for-word from the King James Version of the Bible. So if some of it sounds like "gospel truth," it's probably because parts of it actually are straight out of the Gospels in the New Testament, and other portions are borrowed from the Old Testament.[10]

Third, according to the Bible there are real spiritual forces that oppose what is good—and these could be bringing a deceptive influence as well.[11] We'll discuss this more later, but even a remote possibility of deception ought to give us pause before we assume that a burning sensation, a feeling of emotional warmth, or even the awareness of a spiritual presence in the room automatically means that something is true, or that we should join a particular religion.

The Bible warns us to "test everything that is said. Hold on to what is good. Stay away from every kind of evil."[12] What's interesting about this admonition to "test everything" is that it comes immediately after some verses that say, "Do not stifle the Holy Spirit. Do not scoff at prophecies."[13] So the Bible does not rule out a possible mystical apprehension of truth; in fact, it tells us we should stay open to what God might be saying, even through direct, mystical means. But we must be very careful. Before we embrace new claims, we must test them against what we already know to be true.

How can we do this? One way is to apply this triple test: make sure that the message being given through the mystical encounter is (1) true to the world; (2) true to the messenger's own words; and ultimately, (3) true to God's words.

First, and most obviously, if the new teachings are contrary to established facts in the world or claim a bunch of new ideas that aren't supported by known evidence, then warning buzzers ought to sound. An example would be the Mormon claims about entire civilizations existing in the

Americas—claims that are not supported by history, archaeology, or DNA testing.[14] Or the Muslim assertions we looked at earlier—that Jesus never said he was the Son of God, didn't die on the cross, and therefore did not rise from the dead.[15] The historical record shows us otherwise.

Second, we should look for internal inconsistencies to determine whether leaders or organizations are consistent with their own words. Examples in Mormonism, for instance, include the contradictory accounts that Joseph Smith Jr. gave of his original vision;[16] the unfulfilled prophecies he boldly declared as messages from the Lord; the hundreds of changes quietly made in later editions of the Book of Mormon— many of which radically changed the original meaning; and the largely suppressed evidence of Mormonism's historical racism against dark-skinned people.[17] This racism was part of their doctrine all the way up until 1978 when, under public pressure, they received "new revelations" telling them to change their long-held prejudicial views and practices.[18] Similarly, the Watchtower Society, which is the leadership body over Jehovah's Witnesses worldwide, has characteristically played down, rationalized, or covered up their many false prophecies.[19]

Third, a great model for testing spiritual encounters and teachings is seen in the early days of Christianity, when some new church leaders were still being scrutinized. One of those was Paul, who was a traveling teacher along with a colleague named Silas. Listen to how one group of Christians responded: "The people of Berea were more open-minded than those in Thessalonica, and they listened eagerly to Paul's message." They were open to what God might be saying to them through Paul's teaching, but they didn't exhibit blind trust. Instead, it says, "They searched the Scriptures day after day to see if Paul and Silas were teaching the truth."[20]

In effect, these people were saying, "We like what these men are proclaiming—it all feels pretty good to us—but we're not going to take it on feelings alone. We're going to check it out. We'll test these new teachings against what we know to be established truth. Their message has to be true to God's words." So the Bereans tested the alleged new revelations from Paul against the known and trusted older revelations in the Old Testament Scriptures.

Paul taught this same principle himself. He wrote in his letter to the church in Galatia, "Even if we or an angel from heaven should preach a gospel other than the one we preached to you, let him be eternally condemned! As we have already said, so now I say again: If anybody is preaching to you a gospel other than what you accepted, let him be eternally condemned!"[21] Paul is warning his readers to test every teacher, *including Paul himself,* to carefully weigh what those teachers say against what they already knew to be true from the Scriptures they had (the Old Testament, the teachings of Jesus, and the writings and teachings of the other apostles).

Even though Paul was an apostle himself, he says that we should not automatically trust someone just because he or she claims to be an apostle. Instead, we need to compare their message to the message that has previously been received, knowing that God might reveal things that are new—but he will never contradict what he has already said.

⸻ → ← ⸻

Let's apply this third test to our example of Mormonism and its Mystical approach to faith, keeping in mind that Mormons claim the Bible as part of their lineup of authoritative religious books. What we discover very quickly when we look in the Bible is that it does not teach a "pray and see if it feels right" methodology.[22] On the contrary, it presents a strong principle that says, in effect, don't even consider accepting or doing—and don't pray and ask God about—things he has already made it clear he's against.

For example, look at the story in the Gospel of Matthew when Jesus was fasting in the wilderness:

> The devil took [Jesus] to the holy city, Jerusalem, to the highest point of the Temple, and said, "If you are the Son of God, jump off! For the Scriptures say, 'He will order his angels to protect you. And they will hold you up with their hands so you won't even hurt your foot on a stone.'"
>
> Jesus responded, "The Scriptures also say, 'You must not test the LORD your God.'"[23]

It's interesting that the devil not only tried to tempt Jesus, but he quoted from the Bible in an attempt to back up his position. Yet it is clear he was urging Jesus to do something that was out of God's will. So Jesus called him on it, warning the devil not to test the Lord. Jesus didn't need to pray about it, consult the Scriptures, or talk with anyone in the religious hierarchy. He knew that Satan's request was out of line, so he rejected it immediately.

Let me illustrate this principle in contemporary terms. Let's say you buy a new sports car and are tempted to see if it will really do the top speed the manufacturer claims it will—on a highway with a speed limit of 65. Or you're married, but tempted to get involved with someone at work who is not your spouse. Or your taxes are due and you're going to owe more than you expected, so you're tempted to "adjust" the numbers to make the final amount a little more manageable.

In any of these scenarios, can you imagine having the audacity to stop and pray, "Dear Lord, just this once I want to drive 195 miles an hour on the highway; you'd be okay with that, wouldn't you?" or "Father, that new person at the office is amazingly nice and . . . well . . . good looking—a true testament to your divine creativity. Wouldn't it be okay if we hooked up once or twice?" or "God, the government is terribly wasteful of our tax money, so would it be okay if this one time I tweaked the numbers on my return a bit, just to cut down on some of that governmental waste and put the money to better use?"

I certainly hope you wouldn't ask God to endorse any of those ideas. Because if you did, I think his response would be something like, "Are you kidding me? Don't you already know what I've said about these things? You must not test the Lord your God!"

And yet—this might surprise you—when you understand the broader picture, the challenge to pray to determine whether Mormon teaching is correct is very similar to these examples. Let me explain.

This is often not known by the general public, but

Mormon teachings clearly assert that there are many gods—though we are to worship only one of those gods, the one who is over this world. But that god had a father and mother god, and each of them had parents, and so forth, with the total count of gods numbering into the millions. Further, Mormon theology affirms that every faithful Mormon man can become a god himself and someday be lord over his own planet, producing with his wife (or wives) spirit children who will someday also become gods.

Joseph Smith Jr., the founder of the Church of Jesus Christ of Latter-Day Saints, taught these things very clearly, as did the church's next leader, Brigham Young. In 1840, Lorenzo Snow, the church's fifth president, summed it up with a memorable phrase that has been echoed in Mormon circles ever since: "As man is, God once was; as God is, man may become."[24]

Some Mormon teachers today seem to be distancing themselves from these foundational teachings of their founders, prophets, and leaders. I find that some Mormons I talk to defend this doctrine, while others try to dodge it by saying, "I don't know anything about that." (I've actually gotten *both* of these responses within moments of each other during the same roundtable discussion—from two different Mormons. I said to the second one, the one who had just denied knowledge of the many-gods doctrine, "Of course you know something about it—your friend here just defended it a few minutes ago.")

Even Mormon apologist Robert L. Millet, as recently as 2004, affirmed these doctrines when he wrote, "Latter-day scriptures state unequivocally that God is a man, a Man of

Holiness (Moses 6:57), who possesses a body of flesh and bones (D&C 130:22). . . . What do we know beyond the truth that God is an exalted Man? What do we know of his mortal existence? What do we know of the time before he became God? Nothing. We really do not know more than what the Prophet Joseph Smith stated, and that is precious little."[25]

So let me sum this up: in Mormonism, you have a belief in many gods, though only one of them is actually to be worshiped.[26] This god is a changing being, who used to be a man but progressed over time toward godhood, just as faithful Mormon males seek to do today.

But Mormonism is a faith that also claims to believe the Bible. The problem is that the Bible quite clearly challenges and refutes these central Mormon teachings. Here are a few examples:

"I alone am God. There is no other God—there never has been, and there never will be. . . . You are witnesses that I am the only God," says the LORD. "From eternity to eternity I am God."[27]

"There is no other God but me, a righteous God and Savior. There is none but me. Let all the world look to me for salvation! For I am God; there is no other."[28]

"I am the LORD, and I do not change."[29]

Now, as I affirmed in an earlier chapter, we need to be tolerant of others and support their right to believe and teach their religious points of view. But as lovers of truth, we also need to uphold our own right to respectfully challenge those viewpoints.

Therefore, in light of the vastly contrasting message between the polytheistic (many gods) teachings of Mormonism and the monotheistic (one God) teachings of the Bible, I, for one, would reject the challenge to get on my knees and ask God if the Book of Mormon and the Mormon faith are true.[30] I already know through the teachings of the Bible, which the Mormon faith purports to accept, that many of the core claims of Mormonism are *not* true.

Or put another way, based on the teachings of the Bible, it seems clear that in this case what many people say they "feel" does not equate to something that's "real."

Now let's look at a second guideline for how we can assess mystical encounters:

REAL ≠ GOOD

Even if the first test is passed and you become convinced that what you feel is actually real, the fact that it's real does not necessarily mean that it's good.

Paul illustrated this principle in the letter we looked at earlier, when he said, "Even if we *or an angel from heaven should preach a gospel other than the one we preached to you, let him be eternally condemned!*"[31] In other words, don't automatically accept a message you receive through a mystical experience—even if that experience is in the form of a very real angelic being standing right in front of you—unless it passes the test by bringing a message consistent with what you already know to be true from God's previous revelation in the Bible. Why? Because the angel might be real, but that doesn't mean it's one of God's angels.

In another letter, Paul was more explicit: "Even Satan disguises himself as an angel of light. So it is no wonder that his servants also disguise themselves as servants of righteousness. In the end they will get the punishment their wicked deeds deserve."[32] The apostle John strongly echoed these concerns when he wrote, "Dear friends, do not believe every spirit, but test the spirits to see whether they are from God, because many false prophets have gone out into the world."[33]

This principle of Real ≠ Good played out for me years ago when I was teaching a class of a couple of hundred people, many of whom were in the process of deciding what they should believe. I had been warning about some of the errors of the so-called New Age movement, and that night I had focused on the deceptive and often dangerous practice of fortune-telling. I shared, based on evidence and firsthand studies, how most of what happens in fortune-telling is either fake or explainable through ordinary human perception (and sometimes through old-fashioned trickery). But then I added that it is possible that some psychics are aided with insights and knowledge from spiritual forces—*real* ones, but not *good* ones.

I finished my teaching and asked if anyone had questions about what I'd taught. A woman stood in the back of the room and, to my surprise, announced that she was a professional psychic. Then she challenged me: "You can say anything you want about whether what I do is right or wrong, but I'm here to tell you that it works and that I have insights that couldn't be discovered through any ordinary human means. It's a spiritual power, and it's real."

I took a deep breath and thanked her for coming to the class, as well as for reinforcing the last point I had made—that though much in the world of psychic phenomena, fortune-telling, and sorcery is mere intuition or deception, there are real supernatural powers that can work through these practices. She smiled affirmatively.

But then I cautioned her: "Although these spiritual powers might be real, they're definitely not good." I then reminded her of the biblical warnings, such as those from the apostles Paul and John, as well as some of the clear condemnations of occult practices in the Old Testament.[34] I don't know whether my admonition influenced her or not, but you'd better believe that the rest of the class was paying close attention at that point!

I hope these two guidelines serve you well, at least as first steps in thinking about mystical claims and encounters:

FEEL ≠ REAL

and

REAL ≠ GOOD

Before we end this chapter, let me assure you of something you might not expect: mystical encounters are experiences we will sometimes *feel*, they can be *real*, and they are often *good*—but only when they come from the living God as a way to communicate his love, truth, encouragement, or guidance to us.

I've spent most of this chapter laying out cautions and tests. I needed to do this because so many people are misled by mystical experiences, either imagined or real but dangerous. More than that, our goal is to find a confident faith—one that is based on a firm foundation of facts and spiritual realities. Spiritual encounters of the kind we've been discussing can contribute powerfully to the sense of certainty in what we believe, but only if they're vetted carefully to make sure we're trusting the right messages. For more on how to have that certainty, read the next chapter, on the Evidential faith path.

Let me close now with a few examples of encounters that I think we should celebrate because they pass the various tests, and their claims are corroborated by other kinds of evidence. More than that, they square with what God has told us in his revelation the Bible.

1. The apostle Paul, when he was still known as Saul, had an unexpected encounter with God:

Saul was uttering threats with every breath and was eager to kill the Lord's followers. So he went to the high priest. He requested letters addressed to the synagogues

in Damascus, asking for their cooperation in the arrest
of any followers of the Way he found there. He wanted
to bring them—both men and women—back to
Jerusalem in chains.

As he was approaching Damascus on this mission,
a light from heaven suddenly shone down around him.
He fell to the ground and heard a voice saying to him,
"Saul! Saul! Why are you persecuting me?"

"Who are you, lord?" Saul asked.

And the voice replied, "I am Jesus, the one you are
persecuting! Now get up and go into the city, and you
will be told what you must do."

The men with Saul stood speechless, for they heard
the sound of someone's voice but saw no one! Saul picked
himself up off the ground, but when he opened his eyes
he was blind. So his companions led him by the hand to
Damascus. He remained there blind for three days and
did not eat or drink. . . .

Ananias went and found Saul. He laid his hands
on him and said, "Brother Saul, the Lord Jesus, who
appeared to you on the road, has sent me so that you
might regain your sight and be filled with the Holy
Spirit." Instantly something like scales fell from Saul's
eyes, and he regained his sight. Then he got up and was
baptized. Afterward he ate some food and regained his
strength.[35]

2. Saint Augustine, before he was in any way saintly,
    struggled with temptation and with what to do
    with his life:

I was overcome with anger with myself, knowing what I needed to do but seemingly not able to do it. I gave way to my tears, and in my misery I cried out to [God] in bitter sorrow.

All at once I heard a young child's voice from a nearby garden singing over and over, "Take it and read, take it and read." I looked up, dried my tears, telling myself that this could only be a divine message intended for me to open the Scripture and read what I should find there. I hurried to find the book of Paul's writings, and there opened to Romans 13:13-14. "Not in reveling and drunkenness, not in lust and wantonness, not in quarrels and rivalries. Rather, arm yourselves with the Lord Jesus Christ; spend no more thought on nature and nature's appetites."

In a moment all the darkness of doubt was dispelled and the light of confidence flooded my soul.[36]

3. Blaise Pascal, the eminent French mathematician, wrote an in-the-moment account as he powerfully experienced God's presence during what came to be known as *la nuit de feu*—the Night of Fire:

From about half past ten in the evening until about half past midnight: FIRE.

The God of Abraham, the God of Isaac, the God of Jacob. Not of the philosophers and intellectuals.

Certitude, certitude, feeling, joy, peace!

The God of Jesus Christ. My God and your God . . .

*Forgetfulness of the world and of everything except
God . . .*

The grandeur of the human soul.

*Oh just Father, the world has not known you, but I
have known you. Joy, joy, joy, tears of joy . . .*[37]

Perhaps you, too, have had, or will have, some kind of a
mystical encounter. If so, let me encourage you, in the words
of the apostle Paul—who spoke out of his own experience,
as well as from God's wisdom—not to scoff at it, but to "test
everything that is said. Hold on to what is good. Stay away
from every kind of evil."[38]

CHAPTER EIGHT

THE EVIDENTIAL FAITH PATH:

"Truth Is What Logic and Evidence Point To"

The student Doko came to a Zen master and said, "I am seeking the truth. In what state of mind should I train myself, so as to find it?"

Said the master, "There is no mind, so you cannot put it in any state. There is no truth, so you cannot train yourself for it."

"If there is no mind to train, and no truth to find, why do you have these monks gather before you every day to study Zen and train themselves for this study?"

"But I haven't an inch of room here," said the master, "so how could the monks gather? I have no tongue, so how could I call them together or teach them?"

"Oh, how can you lie like this?" asked Doko.

"But if I have no tongue to talk to others, how can I lie to you?" asked the master.

Then Doko said sadly, "I cannot follow you. I cannot understand you."

"I cannot understand myself," said the master.

A monk came to the master Nansen and asked, "Tell me, is there some teaching that no master has ever taught?"

Nansen said, "There is."

The monk asked, "Can you tell me what it is?"

Nansen said, "It is not Buddha. It is not things. It is not thinking."

Little Toyo was only a twelve-year-old pupil at the Kennin temple, but he wanted to be given a koan to ponder, just like the more advanced students. So one evening at the proper time, he went to the room of Mokurai, the master, struck the gong softly to announce his presence, bowed, and sat before the master in respectful silence.

Finally the master said: "Toyo, show me the sound of two hands clapping."

Toyo clapped his hands.

"Good," said the master. "Now show me the sound of one hand clapping."

Toyo was silent. Finally he bowed and left to consider this problem.

The next night he returned and struck the gong with

one palm. "That is not right," said the master. The next night Toyo returned and played geisha music with one hand. "That is not right," said the master. The next night Toyo returned and imitated the dripping of water. "That is not right," said the master. The next night Toyo returned and imitated the cricket scraping his leg. "That is still not right," said the master.

For ten nights Toyo tried new sounds. At last he stopped coming to the master. For a year he thought of every sound, and discarded them all, until finally he reached enlightenment.

He returned respectfully to the master. Without striking the gong, he sat down and bowed. "I have heard sound without sound," he said.[1]

Does this all make sense to you? If it doesn't—in case you're not initiated into the world of Zen Buddhism and its paradoxical stories called *koans*—here's a Zen "explanation" of that last one:

> *Silence is not silence and sound is not sound. In Zen you can find silence in sound and sound in silence. The sound is always there and the silence is always there, they are THE SAME. Get rid of DEFINITIONS of what silence is and what sound is. Drop conventional thinking and listen when you see a hand. That will lead to understanding of Zen which is freedom.*[2]

Aren't you glad they cleared that up?

Actually, if you're left scratching your head, that's probably a good thing. These little riddles are designed to make us realize the limitations and ultimate futility of logical reasoning. The goal is to help us give up on analytical thought altogether—which is regarded as a vital step toward enlightenment.

Many view this as a hallmark of Eastern thinking; logic as we know it is somehow "Western" and doesn't apply to those living in an Eastern culture. They allegedly see beyond our limited realm of logic, as well as the illusory physical world of maya, and operate on a higher, more spiritual plane.

Intriguing as that might sound, this bifurcated, East vs. West understanding of the world has serious problems. These flaws are illustrated by a story about Ravi Zacharias, a Christian leader who lives in the United States but was raised in India, when he gave a talk at an American university.

Ravi was assailed by one of the university's professors for not understanding Eastern logic. During the Q & A period the professor charged, "Dr. Zacharias, your presentation about Christ claiming and proving to be the only way to salvation is wrong for people in India because you're using 'either–or' logic. In the East we don't use 'either–or' logic—that's Western. In the East we use 'both–and' logic. So salvation is not *either* through Christ *or* nothing else, but *both* Christ *and* other ways."

Ravi found this very ironic because, after all, he grew up in India. Yet here was a Western-born American professor telling Ravi that he didn't understand how things really worked in India! This was so intriguing that Ravi accepted the professor's invitation to lunch in order to discuss it further.

One of the professor's colleagues joined them for lunch, and as he and Ravi ate, the professor used every napkin and placemat on the table to make his point about the two types of logic—one Western and one Eastern.

"There are two types of logic," the professor kept insisting.

"No, you don't mean that," Ravi kept replying.

"I absolutely do!" maintained the professor.

This went on for better than thirty minutes, the professor lecturing, writing, and diagramming. He became so engrossed in making his points that he forgot to eat his meal, which was slowly congealing on his plate.

Upon finishing his own meal, Ravi interrupted. "Professor, I think we can resolve this debate very quickly with just one question."

Looking up from his furious drawing, the professor paused and said, "Okay, go ahead."

Ravi leaned forward, looked directly at the professor, and asked, "Are you saying that when I'm in India, I must use *either* the 'both–and logic' *or* nothing else?"

The professor looked blankly at Ravi, who then repeated his question with emphasis: "Are you saying that when I'm in India, I must use *either*," Ravi paused for effect, "the 'both–and logic' *or*," another pause, "nothing else?"

After glancing sheepishly at his colleague, the professor looked down at his congealed meal and mumbled, "The *either–or* does seem to emerge, doesn't it?" Ravi added, "Yes, even in India we look both ways before we cross the street because it is *either* me *or* the bus, not both of us!"[3]

Logic really is inescapable. Both sides of a contradiction cannot be true—on either side of the ocean. The intellectual conundrums of the Zen teacher or Eastern guru may confound some folks with their mix of cleverness and nonsense, but they certainly do not defeat logic.

In reality, these riddles were *logically* constructed to appear as if they defeat rational thinking. Why? The claim, as we saw above, is that this is to help people let go of logic and move toward some kind of esoteric experience called enlightenment. But what these stories actually do, if anything, is confuse people to the point where they give up on their *own* thinking and accept the *guru's* rationale instead. In the end, logic is not vanquished; it's just a question of *whose* "logic"— and thus whose leadership and influence—will prevail.

In fact, apart from using so-called Western logic, which the Zen koans are meant to defeat, no one would be able to understand anything about these self-contradictory stories. For example, regardless of what the teacher might want to say about the sound or non-sound supposedly made by the one hand clapping, he is still relying on the mind of his student to logically understand what a *hand* is (and not confuse it with a *walrus* or a *Ping-Pong ball*), what it means to *clap* (versus *parachute* or *hiccup*), and what is being discussed when he uses the word *sound* (rather than *appear, taste, smell, feel,* or *itch*). The very definitions of these words—and even the mental thoughts formed before the words are spoken— depend on the logical mind understanding that you're talking about these specific things and actions rather than any others.

Even the incomprehensible admonition we quoted earlier, telling us to "get rid of definitions," presumes that the one receiving those instructions (as well as the one giving them) understands the correct definition of *definitions*, as well as what is entailed in trying to get rid of something.

What all this means is that, in effect, the Eastern teacher must first borrow from so-called Western logic before trying to undermine it—which, of course, is thoroughly self-defeating. And when it comes to finding a confident faith, it's an exceedingly bad idea to base it on any point of view that is self-defeating or that illogically tries to downplay the importance of logic.

In contrast to this, let's examine the sixth and final approach to figuring out our beliefs—which we'll describe as the *Evidential* faith path. This approach involves the careful use of two inescapable faculties God has given us as humans: logic and experience. These include the reasoning of the mind (which we've been discussing) combined with real-world, factual information that we gain through our five senses. Renowned philosopher and theologian William Lane Craig eloquently sums up this approach:

> *Logic and facts are the keys to showing soundly that a conclusion is true. Since a proposition that is logically contradictory is necessarily false and so cannot be the conclusion of a sound argument, and since a proposition validly inferred from factually true premises ought to be regarded as factually true, one may generalize these notions to say that a worldview ought to be regarded as true only if it is logically consistent and fits all the facts known in our experience.*[4]

For the record, the use of these two elements, logic and facts, was at one time divided into two distinct approaches. That was when the rationalists of Continental Europe—mostly under the influence of René Descartes (of "I think, therefore I am" fame)—competed for philosophical dominance with the British empiricists, especially David Hume.

The argument from the rationalist point of view was that the senses can't be trusted, so real knowledge is limited to the logical and mathematical. Just consider, these folks would say, the simple phenomenon of a stick appearing to be bent when you put it partway into water. Your eyes tell you it's crooked, but your rational mind knows better. Therefore logic wins over sensory data.

The empiricists, on the other hand, would counter that the logical mind neither knows nor proves anything without engaging in the real world. Even the bent-stick problem is solved by either feeling the stick to confirm that it is still straight or by pulling it out of the water and looking at it again to see that it's not crooked. Either way, they would say, sensory investigation wins over rational theorizing.

This debate went on for about a century (only philosophers can debate things like this for *that* long). Finally, along came a German thinker named Immanuel Kant, who proposed what would seem to be an obvious solution (as you're reading this with your *eyes* and thinking about it with your *mind*). Kant observed that we need *both*. Real knowledge comes when the logical, organizing power of the mind is applied to the real-world experience gained through the senses. These two elements are fundamental, undeniable realities. To even try to argue against them, you must first employ them. And apart from them, nothing could be known.

Okay, feet back on the ground: How is this Evidential approach applied in real life—and specifically toward finding a faith in which we can be confident?

First, the *logical aspect* forms a primarily negative screen by which an argument is tested (I say "negative screen" because something can be logical but not true, but if it is illogical then it definitely can't be true. Logic is therefore much more readily used to do the latter—show things to be untrue). We've been applying this test to a variety of religious truth claims throughout this book, including my efforts to show the self-defeating contradictions of Zen Buddhism and Eastern thought.

We've also applied the law of noncontradiction to the claims of Islam, whose leaders say that they (1) believe in Jesus and his teachings as a true prophet of God, but (2) deny Jesus' own prophetic claims regarding his identity as the Son of God, his death on the cross, and his resurrection from the dead. Similarly, we've scrutinized the Mormon claim to (1) believe and teach the truths of the Bible, yet (2) teach polytheism (belief in the existence of many gods), which contradicts the consistent monotheistic teachings of the Bible (belief in only one God).

One more example, which we haven't discussed previously, is the claims of the Baha'i religion when it states that

(1) Islam and its teachings are true; (2) Christianity and its teachings are also true (these include, apparently, both sides of the conflicting statements from Islam and Christianity about Jesus' identity, death, and resurrection); (3) Judaism is true as well, including the hope in a not-yet-seen Messiah (who is also, according to Baha'i teachings, the return of Christ for the Christians—which leaders of both Christianity and Judaism reject for their own reasons); and (4) each of these, and several other religions as well, are all true and all fit under the doctrines of Bahaism (which at various points contradicts all the religions it claims to unite, while they all contradict each other).

Whew—it seems that the Baha'i faith earns the dubious honor of being most rationally incoherent of all the religions. So *let the buyer beware*. Having logical contradictions at the heart of a religion's teachings is not just a problem—it is self-defeating to the entire belief system and ought to eliminate it from the consideration of anyone looking for a confident faith.

Now, second, let's look at the flip side of the coin: *sensory experience*. This aspect—which wields the weapons usually described as *facts* or *evidence*—can be used to investigate a faith claim and show it to be false (where it touches on facts related to the tangible world, as opposed to the purely mystical). It can also be used to build a positive case, as I'll show in later chapters.

In terms of discrediting or affirming truth claims, experiential tests can be applied through a variety of disciplines. The most obvious is *general science*, which tests theories and beliefs with physical observation and experimentation. (An example we discussed in the religious realm was whether DNA testing supports the claims in the Book of Mormon that Native Americans are of Middle Eastern descent— which it does not.) In our culture, the observation-and-experimentation approach has become so synonymous with knowledge and education that, for most people, the word *scientific* has come to mean that something is tested, reliable, and therefore almost certainly true. The public's level of trust probably goes beyond what is warranted, especially when we understand that scientific study can offer only varying levels of probability, not absolute proof. But the trust tends to be there just the same.

When we want to investigate claims related to the past, we look to *history*, which is based on events as they were experienced and recorded by people who were actually there, or later by historians using the most reliable records available to them. Much of our knowledge is based on historical accounts, which can be used to confirm or contradict various religious writings and teachings. (For example, written records that report what Jesus claimed about his identity and mission, as well as details related to his death and resurrection.)

I might add that there has been growing skepticism in our culture about the trustworthiness of historical knowledge. This is especially true after some disillusioning revelations have surfaced in recent years, like the discovery that George Washington probably did *not* chop down a cherry tree and then nobly confess, "Father, I cannot tell a lie; I did it with my little hatchet." (If you hadn't heard that this story has been discredited, I'm sorry to have to be the one to break it to you!) If we can't believe classic stories like this one—which we have been taught since childhood—then what historical claims *can* we trust?

Before we disparage the usefulness of history or any of these other disciplines, though, let's remember that it is often the further application of the same discipline that brings us the more accurate answer. For example, in our earlier discussion of the bent-stick illusion, the very senses that tricked the eyes about the stick in the water were the same senses that, with further investigation, brought better information and straightened out our understanding. Similarly, the craft of history that inadvertently taught us the myth about George Washington is the same craft that brought us further and more accurate information, clearing away the myth. It was *historians* who helped to straighten out the historical record. What we need is not the denial of historical knowledge but extra vigilance and care in investigating the facts that undergird any historical record.

Archaeology is another discipline that can give us relevant information about faith-related truth claims. In fact, archaeological research has repeatedly reinforced and confirmed biblical claims from both the Old and New Testaments. The following story about the once-doubted existence of the Hittite nation is one of many examples that could be cited:

> *The Hittites played a prominent role in Old Testament history. They interacted with biblical figures as early as*

Abraham and as late as Solomon. They are mentioned in Genesis 15:20 as people who inhabited the land of Canaan. First Kings 10:29 records that they purchased chariots and horses from King Solomon. The most prominent Hittite is Uriah, the husband of Bathsheba. The Hittites were a powerful force in the Middle East from 1750 B.C. until 1200 B.C. Prior to the late nineteenth century, nothing was known of the Hittites outside the Bible, and many critics alleged that they were an invention of the biblical authors.

In 1876, a dramatic discovery changed this perception. A British scholar named A. H. Sayce found inscriptions carved on rocks in Turkey. He suspected that they might be evidence of the Hittite nation. Ten years later, more clay tablets were found in Turkey at a place called Boghaz-koy. German cuneiform expert Hugo Winckler investigated the tablets and began his own expedition at the site in 1906.

Winckler's excavations uncovered five temples, a fortified citadel and several massive sculptures. In one storeroom he found over ten thousand clay tablets. One of the documents proved to be a record of a treaty between Rameses II and the Hittite king. Other tablets showed that Boghaz-koy was the capital of the Hittite kingdom. Its original name was Hattusha and the city covered an area of 300 acres. The Hittite nation had been discovered![5]

Our *justice system* is also based on an evidential foundation. When someone is on trial, for example, the ultimate questions that matter are not related to theories, suspicions, or prejudices about the person's appearance, past, or proclivities, but to the facts relevant to the actual accusation that can be "proven beyond a reasonable doubt." These are established through reports of what any eyewitnesses saw; sounds a reliable person heard; incriminating evidence found on the scene such as fingerprints, footprints, hair, or blood; written documents and receipts, phone records, bank records, surveillance videos; and so forth. Our society has shown that we have enough confidence in what we can learn from these sensory and experiential data to draw conclusions that allow us to throw people into prison for life—or sometimes even put them to death.

Ordinary observation is also built on the kind of sensory experience we've been discussing. In fact, this is the primary way we learn things day in and day out, sometimes even in the spiritual realm. For example, *Was that person who claims to be healed really sick or impaired in the first place? Does this religious teacher give evidence in his or her life of being a humble, ethical, trustworthy person?* Or even, *Is there any reason to believe this guy riding next to me is really the Holy Spirit?*

So just as we rely on the Evidential approach in ordinary, everyday life, it can also be extremely valuable in the realm of religious understanding. For a relatively small group of people, this is the primary path they've used in figuring out what to believe. For the rest of us, this approach provides us with the keys we need to evaluate the spiritual conclusions we've arrived at through one or more of the other faith paths—as we'll see in chapter 9 and the "Twenty Arrows of Truth" section that follows.

But before we move on from this introduction of the Evidential faith path and further apply its lessons in our quest for a confident faith, we need to address a serious problem we face today. This challenge is one that, left unanswered, could severely limit how we apply the powerful information gained through logic and experience. You see, somewhere along the way, some leading thinkers in our society have moved away from the general use and application of scientific knowledge and toward an ideology that determines in advance what kinds of conclusions will be deemed acceptable within the intellectual community. In effect, these people hijacked science—which historically had been dominated by people of faith—and transformed it into something else, often referred to as scientism, "the belief that the scientific method is the only method for discovering truth."[6]

The doctrine behind scientism, and its narrower expression, *logical positivism*, is that only naturalistic factors (as opposed to supernatural ones) will be considered as possible causes or explanations, regardless of the strength of the evidence presented. In effect, it is an attempt to decide by decree that science will be, from this point forward, atheistic. By definition, God and all things spiritual are ruled out, in advance, from even being considered.

Here's how this plays out on a practical level: someone claims to have been miraculously healed—but the experts have decided in advance that supernatural healings don't happen, so they'll figure out an alternative theory about what occurred, based on purely natural causes.

Or here's another example: eyewitnesses have written down clear and compelling testimonies concerning the miracles of Jesus—especially about his resurrection—but because proponents of scientism have already decided that miracles are mere myths and fairy tales, they'll investigate to find the real story or psychology behind these obviously fanciful claims.

Consider, for example, the commitment to scientism that atheist Richard Dawkins displays at various places in his book *The Blind Watchmaker*:

Biology is the study of complicated things that give the appearance of having been designed for a purpose.[7]

The living results of natural selection overwhelmingly impress us with the appearance of design as if by a master watchmaker, impress us with the illusion of design and planning.[8]

Animals give the appearance of having been designed *by a theoretically sophisticated and practically ingenious physicist or engineer.*[9]

But Dawkins proceeds to write as if it is completely out of the question to even consider the idea that these examples of apparent design could *really* point toward an intelligent designer, as he admits they so clearly and powerfully appear to do. Instead, modeling the mind-set of scientism, he substitutes his own theory, which in reality seems much more improbable: something he describes as "the blind watch-maker." This is Dawkins's term for natural selection, which, he tells us, "is the explanation for the existence and apparently purposeful form of all life, [but] has no purpose in mind. It has no mind and no mind's eye. It does not plan for the future. It has no vision, no foresight, no sight at all."[10]

This pattern runs throughout Dawkins's writings. He exhibits what might best be described as a religious faith in his atheistic assumptions and never gives any real consideration to God, who he claims "*almost* certainly does not exist" as the cause behind anything we observe.[11] It's no wonder that *Harper's* magazine titled its review of Dawkins's latest book as "Hysterical Scientism: The Ecstasy of Richard Dawkins."[12]

So scientism says, in effect, "We've already ruled out the supernatural options on the list of possible explanations; now go ahead and bring us your outlandish claims about gods, angels, and elves, and we'll try to help you sort it all out."

But just imagine for a moment that there is a real God who actually created the world; who did miracles through Jesus, including raising him from the dead; and who chooses at times to show his love and power by healing people of various ailments. (By the way, if God really exists, these things would be mere child's play for him.)

Now, assuming these things were true, and supposing we wanted to be God's advocates, how might we address those scientists and others who have bought into scientism (and ruled out God by definition) in order to persuade them to reconsider their prejudices and see that God is real and truly behind these things?

I don't know the answer, because these folks have already decided to limit their range of possible causes to the realm of the natural, as if science *must*, for some unknown reason or by some unwritten law, exclude any possibility of a super-natural cause.

But how scientific is that? Isn't it the pinnacle of closed-mindedness to say, "Well, even if theoretically there could be a real intelligence in the universe that I don't understand and can't see, I'm resolutely unwilling to consider the possibility of his being involved in the world"? It's like covering your eyes and then complaining that you can't see!

Here's another critical problem: this anti-theistic philosophy does not even live up to its own criteria. When scientism says that the scientific method is the only method for discovering truth, it overlooks the fact that scientism itself cannot be proven scientifically. The scientific method is unable to demonstrate that it is the only method for discovering truth, so the philosophy of scientism fails even by its own standard.

That helps explain what finally happened to logical positivism, which was historically the most articulate expression of scientism. Roy Abraham Varghese, the author of numerous books on the interplay between faith and science, writes:

> As any history of philosophy will show, logical positivism did indeed come to grief by the 1950s because of its internal inconsistencies. In fact, Sir Alfred Ayer himself . . . stated: "Logical positivism died a long time ago. I don't think much of Language, Truth and Logic [Ayer's earlier book that originally taught logical positivism] is true. . . . When you get down to detail,

*I think it's full of mistakes which I spent the last fifty
years correcting or trying to correct.*"[13]

Fascinating turn of events, don't you think? The primary
promoter of logical positivism declaring defeat for his own
scientism-oriented school of thought, along with a confession that the whole system was fraught with problems and
mistakes.

So where does that leave the thinking of scientism today?
Strangely, we're seeing its resurgence in the form of militant
anti-God, antisupernatural, science-oriented books. Varghese
describes this recent phenomenon:

> *The year of the "new atheism" was 2006 (the phrase
> was first used by* Wired *magazine in November 2006).
> From Daniel Dennett's* Breaking the Spell *and Richard
> Dawkins's* The God Delusion *to Lewis Wolpert's* Six
> Impossible Things Before Breakfast, *Victor Stenger's*
> The Comprehensible Cosmos, *and Sam Harris's*
> The End of Faith *(published in 2004, but the sequel
> to which,* Letter to a Christian Nation, *came out in
> 2006), the exponents of a look-back-in-anger, take-no-
> prisoners type of atheism were out in force. . . .*
>
> *The chief target of these books is, without
> question, organized religion of any kind, time, or
> place. Paradoxically, the books themselves read like
> fundamentalist sermons. . . .*
>
> *But how do these works and authors fit into the
> larger philosophical discussion of God of the last several
> decades? The answer is they don't.*

> *In the first place, they refuse to engage the real issues involved in the question of God's existence. . . . Second, they show no awareness of the fallacies and muddles that led to the rise and fall of logical positivism. Those who ignore the mistakes of history will have to repeat them at some point. . . .*
>
> *It would be fair to say that the "new atheism" is nothing less than a regression to the logical positivist philosophy that was renounced by even its most ardent proponents.*[14]

That's a scathing indictment of a seemingly powerful movement—one that is trying to hold science hostage to artificially induced anti-God dogmas. The good news is that we don't have to go along with them. Instead, we can support the growing number of philosophers, scientists, and educators who remain open to *all* of the possible answers to the biggest and most profound questions of our day, including the existence of a divine Creator.

We can also follow the example of the man considered by many to be the leading philosophical atheist of the last generation: the late Antony Flew. Several years before he died, Dr. Flew said, "My life has been guided by the principle of Plato's Socrates: Follow the evidence, wherever it leads."[15] Relentlessly pursuing the evidence, Flew let go of his atheistic beliefs at age eighty-one, publicly embracing the view that there is a God—an intelligent designer—behind the formation of the universe.

Lee Strobel and I had the chance to spend some time with Flew, and we talked with him about these matters. Lee asked him specifically what had prompted such dramatic changes in his point of view. Dr. Flew's response focused on one particular issue: "Einstein felt that there must be intelligence behind the integrated complexity of the physical world. If that is a sound argument, the integrated complexity of the *organic* world is just inordinately greater—all the creatures are complicated pieces of design. So an argument that is important about the physical world is immeasurably stronger when applied to the biological world."[16]

Apparently neither Einstein nor Flew, two of the brightest minds of the past century, had any sense that good science or the Evidential approach was limited to the realm of the natural. And neither should we. Rather, we should embrace and apply the powerful tools of logic and evidence—as we will seek to do for the remainder of this book—employing them in our efforts to find or confirm a faith that squares with the facts.

That is, a faith that is *true*.

CHAPTER NINE

ASSESSING THE SIX FAITH PATHS

At night when all the world's asleep
The questions run so deep
For such a simple man
Won't you please, please tell me what we've learned
I know it sounds absurd
But please tell me who I am

SUPERTRAMP, "THE LOGICAL SONG" [1]

"How do you know that you know what you know?"

My friend Bob Passantino was famous for asking people challenging questions like that—and then keeping them up all hours of the night talking about it. He was relentless. He wouldn't let up on his victims—I mean his *friends*—until they reached clarity or complete exhaustion. Usually, the two came at about the same time. But like some kind of mental workout routine, it was good for me and my intellectual development, as well as for my spiritual growth.

$$\longrightarrow \longleftarrow$$

I'm convinced there's nothing more important than figuring out what we believe about God and his will for our lives.

But I'm also convinced that making wise decisions about our faith involves not only facts and information but also careful consideration concerning how that information will be processed and weighed. We tend to follow one of the six faith paths we've been learning about, and the particular path we choose—or even passively adopt—can have a great bearing on what beliefs we end up embracing.

Since the way we interact with these six paths is so central to the process of finding a confident faith, let's review them, in reverse order from how we originally discussed them, and see what impact each can have on our spiritual journey.

THE EVIDENTIAL FAITH PATH

This sixth path, explained in the previous chapter, is the approach that best tests—and ultimately supports or undermines—all of the others. Its key elements, *logic* and *sensory experience*, are the God-given tools that we use to gain the vast majority of our information, and they are our best resources for examining truth claims and for ultimately deciding what to believe.[2] So we would be well served to grow in these areas—to study logic, working rigorously to think clearly and to scrutinize truth claims to make sure they square with sound reasoning, and to investigate a broad range of information related to our faith, so we can be confident that what we believe is rooted in a solid core of facts and evidence.

Now, I can imagine some fellow Christians insisting I've got it backward. They would say that God's revelation in the Bible has to be primary, setting the standard and testing these other approaches. I actually agree with this—once a person is convinced that the Bible has "passed the test" and proven it is indeed God's true revelation. Then it can and should become the standard by which he or she measures all other truth claims.

But in a world where there are many competing so-called holy books vying for acceptance as God's revelation, we must find a way to put them to the test in order to know which, if any, qualify to be trusted as actual inspired Scripture from God. Short of that you're left with just picking one out arbitrarily, like, for example, the Hindu Bhagavad Gita, or the Book of Mormon—or, yes, maybe the Bible. But if you've arrived at the Bible arbitrarily, you'll lack real conviction when that choice is challenged by a skeptical professor or friend.

So here's the order of thought that I believe can lead to a more confident faith:

- Use logic and evidence to test truth claims, including the claim that the Bible is God's revelation. (If you grew up with that belief, you can confirm it using these tools— thus knowing not just what you believe but also why you believe it.)

- Discover that the Bible alone passes the tests of truth— and accept it as the central authority for your life (including receiving the Savior it presents and his forgiveness and new life).

- Then use the teachings of the Bible to measure and test all other truth claims—but even then you must continue to utilize the God-given tools of logic and evidence to make the comparisons and reach sound conclusions.

THE MYSTICAL FAITH PATH

The fifth approach, explored in chapter 7, can be very powerful because God sometimes uses direct ways to communicate his message to us. But it can also be misleading, if we mistake mere feelings for spiritual realities or we misidentify real but dangerous spiritual entities as being good and from God. We need discernment as well as the willingness to stop and examine what we have experienced. The popular slogan in our culture to "question everything" is actually not far off the mark here. As we've seen, the apostle Paul, who had to examine his own mystical experiences at points along his journey, advises us to "test everything that is said. Hold on to what is good."[3]

"Testing everything" flows from both common sense (including the sixth path's tools of logic and experience) as well as biblical instruction. It involves comparing what you've experienced to what you already know to be true—especially from the Bible, which also gives us this warning:

> Dear friends, do not believe everyone who claims to speak by the Spirit. You must test them to see if the spirit they have comes from God. For there are many false prophets in the world.[4]

That said, if you have a spiritual experience in which God somehow communicates his love or guidance to you—one that passes the tests and proves to be scripturally sound and therefore trustworthy—then you have a great gift that can powerfully impact your life and faith.

THE INTUITIVE FAITH PATH

The fourth approach, which we looked at in chapter 6, can be helpful at least as a warning light indicating that you need to pay attention and investigate further. Hunches and instincts, as well as your inbred conscience, can all build toward a kind of spiritually informed "street smarts" that gives you a sense of what you should do and whom you can trust.

But let me again caution you not to heed your hunches in isolation, apart from other objective criteria. That flashing yellow light in a dark intersection doesn't tell you anything clearly or conclusively. It merely says, *Driver beware*. It prompts you to look into the matter by slowing down, heightening your awareness, scanning the road left and right, and searching for more information that will help you know how to proceed.

That's a pretty good description of the Intuitive approach when it's working right. It calls your attention to danger, or perhaps opportunity, and prompts you to do whatever it takes to inform your mind and further educate your intuition. In other words, it tells you to investigate more deeply and probably to apply the criteria of some of the other faith paths, especially the sixth path, to confirm and clarify the warnings you've received.

So heed the promptings, and look into the reasons behind what you are sensing. Examine the supporting evidence, especially for the spiritual beliefs you embrace. Let your "gut feelings" confirm what you find, but don't let them lead you down a blind alley, stumbling around in the dark and hoping to happen upon truth. Rather, turn on more lights through finding additional, clearer information—and ask God for guidance along the way.

THE AUTHORITARIAN FAITH PATH

The third approach, reviewed in chapter 5, is based on beliefs from an authority figure or organization that are often imposed with the expectation that you will receive them without question. This message can come across in subtle ways, or it can be accompanied by overt threats of relational, financial, or even physical repercussions should you fail to stay in line. Consequently, it often requires courage to examine the qualifications of the authorities in our lives and the ideas they've taught us.

But examine them we must. Authorities, like traditions, often contradict one another in what they teach; therefore, they can't all be correct. And though we all will end up living under some kind of authority, in the spiritual realm we need to test the teachings of those leaders who hold sway over us (or who would like to), to ensure that they are truly worth following.

If you are under a spiritual authority that tries to do all your thinking for you, let me encourage you to step back and start thinking for yourself. Apply the tests of logic and evidence from the sixth path. You really can decide whether or not to let that person or organization keep leading you. But be wise in how you do this. Usually, there's no need to announce that you're reconsidering what you've been taught. Instead, quietly, humbly, and prayerfully begin to examine the evidence that purportedly supports the beliefs you've been handed. Your research might end up confirming the validity of those beliefs and actually reinforcing the credentials of the leadership you're currently under. That would be great because it would give you more confidence in your faith. But it's also possible that you'll find information that leads you to better conclusions and a wiser choice of leaders to follow.

Don't settle for simple answers or cave into authoritarian pressures to simply conform. Jesus, who I believe had the credentials to be accepted as the ultimate authority, urged us to "Keep on asking, and you will receive what you ask for. Keep on seeking, and you will find. Keep on knocking, and the door will be opened to you."[5] He also made a promise to those who would ask, seek, and follow what they learned: "You will know the truth, and the truth will set you free."[6]

THE TRADITIONAL FAITH PATH

This second approach, which we examined in chapter 4, is generally passive, relying on hand-me-down beliefs, habits, or traditions that are only as good as the quality of the thinking that got them started in the first place. They may be right, but they could be wrong, too. You'll never know until you back up and look into the logic and evidence behind the traditional beliefs you were raised with to see which ones are actually valid and therefore worth holding on to.

One thing's for sure: because different faith traditions often contradict one another, they can't all be correct. It's important, therefore, to stop and look at them more deeply. Examining your faith traditions may actually feel inappropriate or disrespectful at first, given family and cultural expectations that you'll just loyally "carry on the traditions." But the hero of the story is never the one who simply goes along with the crowd or passively perpetuates the practices of yesteryear. Rather, the person we admire is the man or woman who has the courage to see things anew, if need be—who embraces what's right and then acts on it.

That said, when you've done due diligence in examining the foundations of your faith and found that its basic tenets are based on truth, then you can more confidently embrace those beliefs—and pass them on as tested traditions to the next generation.

THE RELATIVISTIC FAITH PATH

The first approach, which we discussed back in chapter 3, treats truth as a subjective by-product of the mind—something you invent rather than discover. So as long as you're convinced that what you think determines what's real for you, why not just think things that work for you, serve your needs, and fit with whatever else you've already decided to believe in?

It's not hard to imagine how this mind-over-matter methodology would lead someone to ignore uncomfortable information and choose instead to embrace ideas that seem desirable. So for example, if *what works* is to think that you are your own god, as New Age thinking tells us, or if *what fits* is to decide that morality is merely a by-product of our culture but really not binding on us as individuals, then why not just do whatever feels right?

But where does this approach take you? It promises to take you anywhere you'd like to go—at least in your own mind—but you're probably not going to like the outcome. It's like the person who gets bad reports back from the lab but chooses not to believe in the unpleasantries of cancer and therefore opts to forgo treatment. It's far better to look for, discover, and then deal with the actual truth—*what is*—and find a faith that is built on facts so you can truly face reality.

So again, my encouragement is to step off this path. Instead, search for real truth, and when you find it, grab onto it with both hands and never let go.

Real truth is precisely what my friend Bob Passantino, whom I mentioned at the beginning of this chapter, was looking for. When Bob was young, he was a serious spiritual skeptic who was fully convinced that Christianity was false. In fact, he loved to corner Christians and intimidate them with his challenging questions.

One day Bob tried to pick on the wrong person, a very bright seminary student named Gene Kirby. Gene invited him to come to his home—if he was really serious about getting answers—to discuss the issues. Bob took him up on the offer—not just once, but every Tuesday night for about six months. Bob threw every objection he could think of at Gene, who patiently but persistently gave him good answers. Gradually, Bob began to see that there is solid logic and evidence for the Christian faith.

All of this made Bob begin to reconsider his anti-Christian point of view, but he wasn't ready to change his mind too quickly. He frankly didn't like the limiting effect he thought it would have on his lifestyle. Instead, he broke off contact with Gene, joined the National Guard, and left the area for almost a year. During that time he dabbled in drugs, explored various philosophies, got trained in the martial arts, and even looked into Buddhism.

Then, one day, he had a mystical encounter that rocked his world. He was sitting in his Volkswagen Beetle with a friend named Bruce, discussing their concerns about catastrophic things that could happen to the world and what they could do to be ready. Suddenly, Bob "felt the unmistakable and real presence of the Holy Spirit fill the car. Without sound or words, he clearly heard Jesus speaking to him, saying, 'None of that matters. You are putting your trust in yourselves instead of in Me. All that matters is that I love you. Follow me. . . . Follow me. . . . Follow me.'"[7]

Bob turned to Bruce, hesitating as he tried to figure out how to tell him what he was experiencing. "Bruce, none of this matters," Bob ventured. "Jesus is real."

Much to Bob's surprise, Bruce, who had been experiencing something similar, blurted out, "Don't you feel the Holy Spirit? We have to follow Jesus! He's calling us!" The two of them sat in the car, shocked by what had happened but also enjoying God's presence, until they finally needed to leave.

That day changed Bob's life, though he didn't follow the Mystical path blindly. He knew his experience needed to be tested. He checked it out carefully, including the implications that this encounter might have on his broader beliefs and life.

If you had asked Bob which faith paths helped him on his journey, as I did years later, his answer was the Evidential path (with its mix of logic and real-world data and information) along with a touch of tested Mysticism—which made for a powerful and compelling combination.

When he reached a point of real confidence, Bob committed himself to what he now understood through his divine encounter as well as his pursuit of spiritual truth. He became a fully devoted follower of Christ and immediately began telling his friends what had happened. He also answered their most daunting questions and challenges (most of which they had originally learned from him) with the compelling answers he had so recently discovered himself.

Then Bob, together with his wife, Gretchen, spent the rest of his life helping others in that same search for knowledge and truth. He knew the difference Christ had made in his own life, and he passionately wanted others to experience what *he* had experienced. Perhaps that's why he was so doggedly persistent in prodding others toward the truth.

When Bob died suddenly of heart failure in 2003, Gretchen, their three children, and their many friends—including me— were all in shock. Here's part of what I wrote to honor and remember him in the days immediately after his death:

> *I'm still reeling over the loss of my wonderful friend and mentor of the last twenty-five years, Bob Passantino. I'll miss his wisdom, his encouragement, his partnership, and especially his humor. There's no one else quite like him.* . . .
>
> *It was never a good idea to get on the other side of an argument from Bob—he was RIGHT!*
>
> *You proved it, Bob, through your logic, through your love, and through your life. I, and many others, will be indebted to you throughout eternity.*[8]

It was under Bob's influence, and that of a few other key individuals, including his wife, Gretchen, that I decided to invest my life in helping others find the pathway toward truth—and toward the One who *is* Truth. It's in that spirit that I offer this discussion about how to find a confident faith.

TWENTY
ARROWS
OF TRUTH

Reasons You Can Be Confident the Christian Faith Is True

CHAPTER TEN

HOW SCIENCE AND LOGIC POINT TOWARD SPIRITUAL TRUTH

The heavens proclaim the glory of God.
The skies display his craftsmanship.
Day after day they continue to speak;
night after night they make him known.
They speak without a sound or word;
their voice is never heard.
Yet their message has gone throughout the earth,
and their words to all the world.

PSALM 19:1-4

We've explored the six faith paths and discussed their strengths and weaknesses as avenues for finding trustworthy beliefs. Now, for the next three chapters, I'll present twenty arguments that flow from the most helpful of these approaches, especially the sixth path, that I believe direct us to spiritual truth. Though not every argument will be equally compelling to every reader, together they provide a cumulative case that I'm convinced points powerfully to the unique claims of the Christian worldview.

I'll describe each argument as an *arrow*—because each one points in a certain direction (as we'll see on the diagram in chapter 13). In this chapter, I'll describe reasons that flow from the areas of logic and science. In the following two chapters, we'll focus on evidence related to the Bible, history, and experience.

If you come from a Christian background, I hope these arguments will strengthen your faith—not just because of tradition or authority, but because they hold up factually and logically. If you come from a non-Christian background, I hope you'll carefully consider and weigh these points of evidence, asking for God's guidance as you do. Don't forget the skeptic's prayer, echoing what a man once said to Jesus—"I do believe, but help me overcome my unbelief!"—even if all you can honestly say is the "help my unbelief" part.[1] (Also, be sure to read chapter 13 where we'll discuss the kinds of barriers that can trip us up on our spiritual journeys.)

ARROW 1: DESIGN IN THE UNIVERSE POINTS TO AN *INTELLIGENT DESIGNER.*

This "argument from design" is based on a mix of observation, intuition, logic, and perhaps a dose of common sense. The classic rendition of this comes from William Paley in his book *Natural Theology*, published in 1802. Paley's famous argument states that if you find a watch on the ground, you immediately surmise it is not a fluke of nature. Watches, by virtue of their complexity and design, require a watchmaker. Whenever something shows evidence of having been made for a purpose, it points us back to a purposeful cause behind it, or an intelligent designer.

Two hundred-plus years later, it's still true. Nobody picks up a watch on the beach and says, "Praise the cosmos! Just look at this wonderful creation that the forces of chance have tossed together." But more than that, as my friend Cliffe Knechtle says, "If you think the *watch* needs a designer, just glance from the watch to your *hand*. It is far more complex, has far more moving parts, displays much more intricate design, and therefore demands a designer that much more."

This observation is taken even further in a fascinating description from Michael Denton, an Australian molecular biologist, when he talks about a unit of life far smaller than the human hand:

> *Perhaps in no other area of modern biology is the challenge posed by the extreme complexity and ingenuity of biological adaptations more apparent than in the fascinating new molecular world of the cell. . . . To grasp the reality of life as it has been revealed by molecular biology, we must magnify a cell a thousand million times until it is twenty kilometers in diameter and resembles a giant airship large enough to cover a great city like London or New York. What we would then see would be an object of unparalleled complexity and adaptive design. On the surface of the cell we would see millions of openings, like the port holes of a vast space ship, opening and closing to allow a continual stream of materials to flow in and out. If we were to enter one of these openings we would find ourselves in a world of supreme technology and bewildering complexity. . . .*
>
> *Is it really credible that random processes could have constructed a reality, the smallest element of which— a functional protein or gene—is complex beyond our*

own creative capacities, a reality which is the very antithesis of chance, which excels in every sense anything produced by the intelligence of man?[2]

As breathtaking as that example is, I don't know which is more astounding: the design that is evident when looking down through a microscope or up through a telescope. The realization that the beauty, order, and grandeur of the universe points us to the divine designer goes back at least as far as King David, the Psalm writer, when he said some three millennia ago, "The heavens proclaim the glory of God. The skies display his craftsmanship."[3] Hundreds of years later, the apostle Paul picked up on David's theme and added a challenge: "Ever since the world was created, people have seen the earth and sky. Through everything God made, they can clearly see his invisible qualities—his eternal power and divine nature. So they have no excuse for not knowing God."[4]

Before moving on, it's worth mentioning an objection that has been raised by atheists as far back as David Hume and as recently as Richard Dawkins: "The designer hypothesis immediately raises the larger problem of who designed the designer."[5] In other words he's saying that, at best, design in the universe only points to a finite designer—not an infinite deity.

Three thoughts in response:

1. Even if the existence of a finite designer was all we could deduce from this evidence (which I don't think is the case), this designer must be *extremely old, incredibly intelligent, amazingly powerful,* and *wonderfully wise* to have invented,

designed, and somehow produced all of
what we see in the universe, including its 10
billion galaxies and 70 sextillion stars (that's
70,000,000,000,000,000,000,000—and those
are just the ones we can see).[6] Any being of that
creative magnitude certainly ought to get our
attention, capture our imagination, and would
undoubtedly be worth listening to.

2. We shouldn't stop with the existence of a finite
designer, if that's all we can deduce at first. If the
original fact of design in the universe compels us
to acknowledge a very old, very wise, and very
powerful designer, then that same logic, when
applied to the designer himself, should take us
at least one step further, right?

In other words, if this amazing, but finite,
designer shows such incredible marks of design
himself, then who designed and made him? That
designer-behind-the-designer must be even more
completely mind boggling. And if *that* designer is
limited in any way, we can only imagine (seriously,
we *can't even* imagine) what the being who made
him must be like. If we follow this track back far
enough, it seems we're rapidly approaching an
eternal, omniscient, omnipotent, omnipresent
God. Indeed, the argument from design will
eventually draw us back to an *infinite* designer,
who will probably be uncannily similar to the
God of Abraham, Isaac, and Jacob described in
the Bible.

3. What if this intelligent designer actually went to
    the effort of revealing what he's like in other ways,
    beyond just the clues we see in nature? What if he
    spoke through chosen people, explaining that he's
    not only an intelligent designer but also an eternal,
    all-powerful being who cares about his creatures
    and wants to have a relationship with us?

    If he's all we know he must be, then ought
    we not sit up and take notice regarding whatever
    else he might want to say to us? The evidence
    from design leads us to at least consider potential
    information from revelation.

ARROW 2: FINE-TUNING IN THE UNIVERSE POINTS TO AN INTENTIONAL *FINE-TUNER*.

The design argument has been a strong one for thousands of
years. Its logic and intuitive force are hard to escape. But in
recent years, scientific discovery has turbocharged it. That's
because our growing understanding of numerous *constants*
in physics points to the fine-tuning of the universe in a way
that enables it to support life.

In his book *The Creator and the Cosmos*, astrophysicist
Hugh Ross lists more than two dozen examples of areas
in which the universe had to fall within extremely narrow
tolerances for any kind of life to exist.[7] The chances of
this all happening randomly, he explains, are vanishingly
small.

Robin Collins, author of a chapter on fine-tuning in *God
and Design: The Teleological Argument and Modern Science*,
described the situation in an interview with Lee Strobel:

When scientists talk about the fine-tuning of the universe, they're generally referring to the extraordinary balancing of the fundamental laws and parameters of physics and the initial conditions of the universe. Our minds can't comprehend the precision of some of them. The result is a universe that has just the right conditions to sustain life. The coincidences are simply too amazing to have been the result of happenstance—as [theoretical physicist, cosmologist, and astrobiologist] Paul Davies said, "The impression of design is overwhelming."

I like to use the analogy of astronauts landing on Mars and finding an enclosed biosphere, sort of like the domed structure that was built in Arizona a few years ago. At the control panel, they find that all the dials for its environment are set just right for life. The oxygen ratio is perfect; the temperature is seventy degrees; the humidity is fifty percent; there's a system for replenishing the air; there are systems for producing food, generating energy, and disposing of wastes. Each dial has a huge range of possible settings, and you can see if you were to adjust one or more of them just a little bit, the environment would go out of whack and life would be impossible. What conclusion would you draw from that? . . .

Some intelligent being had intentionally and carefully designed and prepared it to support living creatures. And that's an analogy for our universe.

Over the past thirty years or so, scientists have discovered that just about everything about the basic structure of the universe is balanced on a razor's edge for life to exist. The coincidences are far too fantastic to attribute this to mere chance or to claim that it needs no explanation. The dials are set too precisely to have been a random accident. Somebody, as [astrophysicist and cosmologist] Fred Hoyle quipped, has been monkeying with the physics.[8]

Strobel and Collins went on to talk about a number of amazing examples of the physics having been "monkeyed with." Here's just one of the mind-stretching points they discussed, called the *cosmological constant*, which is the energy density of empty space:

"Well, there's no way we can really comprehend it," Collins said. "The fine-tuning has conservatively been estimated to be at least one part in a hundred million billion billion billion billion billion. That would be a ten followed by fifty-three zeroes. That's inconceivably precise. . . . Let's say you were way out in space and were going to throw a dart at random toward Earth. It would be like successfully hitting a bull's-eye that's one trillionth of a trillionth of an inch in diameter. That's less than the size of one solitary atom."[9]

If the odds are that small for just this one area to be so precisely tuned to support life, imagine how small the odds become when you add in another thirty factors or so. The chances become so small that, as Lee Strobel likes to say, "by comparison, they make the lottery look like a sure bet!"

Former atheist Patrick Glynn, in his book *God: The*

Evidence, sums it up like this: "As recently as twenty-five years ago, a reasonable person weighing the purely scientific evidence on the issue would likely have come down on the side of skepticism."[10] Not anymore, Glynn argues: "Today, the concrete data point strongly in the direction of the God hypothesis. It is the simplest and most obvious solution."[11]

William Paley would have salivated back in 1802 to have this astounding scientific support for his contention that watches require a watchmaker. He simply had no way of knowing how amazing the "watch" of this world really is. But we have that knowledge today, and it's another powerful pointer to the existence of an amazingly wise God who is behind it all—one who must care a lot for his creatures, since he so painstakingly created a habitat suitable for them.

ARROW 3: INFORMATION ENCODED INTO DNA POINTS TO A *DIVINE ENCODER.*

Another compelling example of design comes from the world of biology, specifically the incredible complexity of the information encoded within DNA. Francis Collins, head of the international Human Genome Project that mapped out the entire DNA sequence of the human species, describes it like this:

> *This newly revealed text was 3 billion letters long, and written in a strange and cryptographic four-letter code. Such is the amazing complexity of the information carried within each cell of the human body, that a live reading of that code at a rate of three letters per second would take thirty-one years, even if reading*

continued day and night. Printing these letters out in
regular font size on normal bond paper and binding
them all together would result in a tower the height of
the Washington Monument. For the first time on that
summer morning this amazing script, carrying within
it all of the instructions for building a human being,
was available to the world.[12]

The name of Collins's book says it all: *The Language of*
God—a title that echoes the words of President Bill Clinton
when he stood next to Francis Collins and announced that
the amazing genome project had finally been completed:
"We are learning the language in which God created life."[13]

Why all the theological language at a press conference for
a scientific breakthrough? Because this was not just an amazing human accomplishment; it unveiled the incredible scope
of the actual biological language in which information—
literally, the library of instructions by which living organisms
are put together—is contained and conveyed.

Information is not recorded and communicated by mere
chance. A common illustration contrasts two separate patterns on a beach: one being the ripples in the sand formed by
the waves, and the other, the words *John loves Mary*, written
in the sand. The wave-drawn patterns may be interesting and
even beautiful to look at, but they're randomly formed by
nature. The words *John loves Mary*, however, would never be
mistaken for something random. Clearly they are a message
intended to communicate an idea—one to which John hopes
Mary will be receptive.

But if it is obvious that something as simple as "John

loves Mary" is intelligent communication, how much more so is the life-giving "message" of DNA, which is, as Francis Collins puts it, "3 billion letters long, and written in a . . . four-letter code . . . [that is] our own instruction book, previously known only to God"?[14]

So powerful is this evidence that Dean Kenyon, a biophysicist from San Francisco State University who had coauthored a book trying to explain the emergence of life apart from any supernatural involvement, later made a dramatic turnabout. "Kenyon . . . repudiated the conclusions of his own book, declaring that he had come to the point where he was critical of all naturalistic theories of origins. Due to the immense molecular complexity of the cell and the information-bearing properties of DNA, Kenyon now believed that the best evidence pointed toward a designer of life."[15]

Kenyon sums up his own conclusions when he says, "This new realm of molecular genetics [is] where we see the most compelling evidence of design on the Earth."[16] Kenyon's words echo the opinion of many other leading scientists and thinkers around the world—and I hope an opinion that you share, or will soon adopt as your own: the information encoded in DNA points powerfully to a *Divine Encoder.*[17]

ARROW 4: THE BEGINNING OF THE UNIVERSE POINTS TO A *DIVINE ORIGINATOR.*

The logic is powerful in its simplicity. Consider three statements that make up what is commonly referred to as the *cosmological argument*:

> *Whatever has a beginning has a cause.*
> *The universe had a beginning.*
> *Therefore, the universe had a cause.*[18]

Looking at the first statement, it seems obvious that *whatever has a beginning has a cause*. Few people would argue with this. Albert Einstein declared, "The scientist is possessed by a sense of universal causation."[19] The whole methodology of science involves studying effects in order to discover the causes behind them. In fact, this causal connectedness is another one of those inescapable realities. Don't ask me why this is—because if you do, you'll only be making my point. (You'll be trying to get at the cause behind the effect of my statement, which says effects demand causes.)

My friend Chad Meister illustrates this first statement in a real-life scenario: "If I go to the doctor to find out why a lump has begun growing in my throat, I'm not going to be satisfied with his telling me that there's no cause for that lump—that it just sprang up for no reason, with no real cause. Instead, I'm going to go find a new doctor."

If you're a parent, and you go into one of your kids' rooms and find a hole punched in the wall, you're not going to accept a causeless, self-existent hole-in-the-wall theory. Instead, you want a real explanation from your son or daughter—the old-fashioned kind that actually *explains*.

If you loan someone your car, and he brings it back with a fresh dent in the bumper, you don't want to enter into a philosophical discussion about whether or not "dents that begin to exist need a cause"; you just want to know what your friend ran into—and how he's going to pay for the repairs.

If the sudden appearance of lumps, holes, and dents needs a cause, how much more so the original materialization of the universe?

The second statement in the argument claims that *the universe had a beginning.* The only other option is to say that it is eternal and has simply always been there—an answer akin to the causeless, self-existent hole-in-the-wall theory, or to claim that it popped into existence out of nothing and from nothing: *poof.* But as author Norman Geisler winsomely makes clear by quoting the lyrics of a song from *The Sound of Music,* "Nothing comes from nothing, nothing ever could." We really do know better.[20]

So we know through commonsense logic that the universe had a beginning—but we know it through modern science, as well. Robert Jastrow, an astronomer and the founding director of NASA's Goddard Institute for Space Studies, summarized the conclusion of decades of scientific research in his groundbreaking book *God and the Astronomers:* "Five independent lines of evidence—the motions of the galaxies, the discovery of the primordial fireball, the laws of thermodynamics, the abundance of helium in the Universe and the life story of the stars—point to one conclusion; all indicate that the Universe had a beginning."[21]

Jastrow also explains the theory of that amazing beginning, usually referred to in scientific circles as the big bang:

> The matter of the Universe is packed together into
> one dense mass under enormous pressure, and with
> temperatures ranging up to trillions of degrees. The

dazzling brilliance of the radiation in this dense, hot Universe must have been beyond description. The picture suggests the explosion of a cosmic hydrogen bomb. The instant in which the cosmic bomb exploded marked the birth of the Universe.

The seeds of everything that has happened in the Universe since were planted in that first instant; every star, every planet and every living creature in the Universe owes its physical origins to events that were set in motion in the moment of the cosmic explosion. In a purely physical sense, it was the moment of creation.[22]

Stephen Hawking, the popular theoretical physicist, adds perspective on how widespread this understanding is in scientific circles: "Almost everyone now believes that the universe, and time itself, had a beginning at the big bang."[23]

So both logic and science tell us that the universe had a beginning. And we established earlier that whatever has a beginning has a cause. So the natural conclusion is that *the universe had a cause.*

But that leaves us with the realization that something *outside of the universe* caused it.[24] That "something" would have to be big enough, smart enough, powerful enough, and old enough—not to mention have enough of a creative, artistic flair—to be able to pull off such a grand "effect." That sounds suspiciously similar to the divine being described in the book of Genesis, which starts with these words: "In the beginning God created the heavens and the earth."[25]

Or, as Robert Jastrow puts it famously at the end of *God*

and the Astronomers, "For the scientist who has lived by his faith in the power of reason, the story ends like a bad dream. He has scaled the mountains of ignorance; he is about to conquer the highest peak; as he pulls himself over the final rock, he is greeted by a band of theologians who have been sitting there for centuries."[26]

For us, however, the dream can end well: science and Scripture converge, pointing in the same direction—toward a *Divine Originator*—as together they assist us in finding a faith we can wholeheartedly embrace.

ARROW 5: THE SENSE OF MORALITY THROUGHOUT THE HUMAN RACE POINTS TO A *MORAL LAWGIVER*.

Each of us has an internal standard of morality—but one that is above us and comes from outside of us. Why do I say that the source of this morality is above and outside us? Because everybody has it, but nobody consistently lives up to it. Why would we each invent a code of ethics that we could never quite fulfill, and then employ it to frustrate and condemn ourselves all life long?

I'm not saying that our standards are exactly the same, just that there is a universal sense of right and wrong that every person possesses. We can't get rid of it, short of becoming so jaded that our "consciences have been seared as with a hot iron."[27] If morality were mere preference or fashion, we could much more easily detach ourselves from it.

C. S. Lewis comments in the opening section of his classic *Mere Christianity*, titled "Right and Wrong as a Clue to the Meaning of the Universe," on this sense of morality, which he calls the Law of Nature:

Whenever you find a man who says he does not believe
in a real Right and Wrong, you will find the same man
going back on this a moment later. He may break his
promise to you, but if you try breaking one to him he
will be complaining "It's not fair" before you can say
Jack Robinson. A nation may say treaties don't matter;
but then, next minute, they spoil their case by saying
that the particular treaty they want to break was an
unfair one. But if treaties do not matter, and if there
is no such thing as Right and Wrong—in other words,
if there is no Law of Nature—what is the difference
between a fair treaty and an unfair one? Have they
not let the cat out of the bag and shown that, whatever
they say, they really know the Law of Nature just like
anyone else?

It seems, then, we are forced to believe in a real
Right and Wrong. People may be sometimes mistaken
about them, just as people sometimes get their sums
wrong; but they are not a matter of mere taste and
opinion any more than the multiplication table.[28]

And just as we learn the multiplication tables from our
parents or teachers, we also learn moral truths from our parents and teachers—but that does not imply that our parents
and teachers *invented* these moral truths.

Some people argue that our moral sense is instilled in us
by the society in which we live. Though that may be partially
true, certain aspects of our moral understanding transcend
culture. Why is it, for example, that even as outsiders to the
Iraqi culture, we intuitively judged as wrong the actions of

Saddam Hussein when we learned that he had murdered family members, tortured and killed people he considered to be political threats, and ordered the gassing of thousands of Kurds? We knew that what he had done to his own people was wrong—period.

And Adolf Hitler? His "final solution" to eliminate the Jewish race may have emanated from his own heartless insanity, but it was soon embraced by many others—not only the leaders but the entire Nazi party and many of its supporters. Yet we do not, and certainly should not, hold back from condemning the Nazis' horrible actions merely because what they did was within the context of their own culture or in line with their own laws.

At the Nuremberg trials after the war, people both inside and outside German society stepped up and judged what had been done within the Nazi culture based on a universal sense of morality. And rightly so. If murdering innocent people is wrong in your own home, certainly it is wrong in your neighbor's home across the street or on the other side of town—and in other countries where they speak different languages. It doesn't matter where one commits murder; it's still wrong.

Yet where did we get this sense of right and wrong? If we didn't invent it, if it transcends the realms of culture and politics, if it's something we can't get away from, then what is its source? Could it be that a *Moral Lawgiver* actually knit those moral standards, along with the ability to understand and operate by them, into the very fabric of what it means to be human?

That conclusion certainly squares with logic and experience. Interestingly, it's also in line with what the Bible tells us:

"They demonstrate that God's law is written in their hearts, for their own conscience and thoughts either accuse them or tell them they are doing right."[29]

The "moral argument" is summed up well by Lee Strobel in *The Case for Faith*:

> *Without God, morality is simply the product of sociobiological evolution and basically a question of taste or personal preference. . . . Without God, there is no absolute right and wrong that imposes itself on our conscience. But we know deep down that objective moral values do exist—some actions, like rape and child torture, for example, are universal moral abominations—and, therefore, this means God exists.*[30]

Our sense of morality really does imply the existence of a *Moral Lawgiver*.

Though much more could be said from the areas of logic and science, the evidence from these arguments alone points strongly toward a *Divine Creator*

- who started this immense universe with a bang;

- who shaped it and all of the creatures in it with incredible detail and design;

- who fine-tuned it to extremely precise tolerances so it would be able to support life, including yours and mine;

- who encoded our DNA with an amazingly complex and comprehensive language; and

- who created us as humans with a pervasive and inescapable sense of morality.

And we're just getting started. Let's look at arguments related to the Bible next.

CHAPTER ELEVEN

HOW EVIDENCE FOR THE BIBLE POINTS TOWARD SPIRITUAL TRUTH

That which was from the beginning, which we have heard, which we
have seen with our eyes, which we have looked at and our hands have
touched—this we proclaim concerning the Word of life.

1 JOHN 1:1 (NIV)

In chapter 10, we explored some of the logical and scientific evidence that points toward the existence of a wise and powerful God—a God who is the cause of the universe and the designer who shaped it to support life. We also saw how he wove his moral standards into the fabric of the human personality, causing us to be aware of the sobering reality that we all fall short of his standard.

In this chapter, we'll examine some of the evidence for the Bible and see how that evidence points to the validity of the Christian faith.

 ARROW 6: THE BIBLE SHOWS ITSELF TO BE A UNIQUELY _CONSISTENT_ RELIGIOUS BOOK.

Despite a growing number of attacks on the Bible in recent years, it still presents strong evidence for its supernatural authorship. How? One way is through its extraordinary *consistency.*

People often talk about the Bible as if it were one book, but it is actually a collection of many books. Yet these documents show amazing unity between those books, as noted by scholars Norman Geisler and William Nix:

> *Composed as it is of sixty-six books, written over a period of some fifteen hundred years by about forty authors using several languages and containing hundreds of topics, it is more than accidental or incidental that the Bible possesses an amazing unity of theme—Jesus Christ.*
>
> *It is only later reflection, both by the prophets themselves (for example, see 1 Peter 1:10-11) and later generations, that has discovered that the Bible is really one book whose "chapters" were written by men who had no explicit knowledge of the overall structure. Their individual roles could be compared to that of different men writing chapters of a novel for which none of them have even an overall outline. Whatever unity the book has must come from beyond them. Like a symphony, each individual part of the Bible contributes to an overall unity that is orchestrated by one Master.*[1]

For example, even though Jesus wasn't born until the time period covered in the New Testament and is therefore never mentioned by name in the Old Testament, he is predicted and discussed—as the coming Messiah—many places in the Old Testament. (I'll cite several examples later in this chapter.)

This degree of consistency would be difficult enough to achieve within a single book by a solo author—but when you add the complexity of multiple writers, from multiple countries, in multiple languages, over multiple centuries, dealing with multiple problems and situations, the Bible's incredible cohesion and unified message are nothing short of miraculous.

The best way to get a sense of this is to spend some time reading the Bible for yourself, preferably in a modern, understandable version.[2] As you read, I think you'll notice the logical integrity, the consistent relevance, the real-world accuracy, and the subjective-but-real "ring of truth" that countless people have affirmed over the years.

By contrast, it's worth pointing out that this high level of logic and clarity is absent from later would-be gospels that some people say should have been part of the biblical canon.[3] For example, after you've spent some time reading the ennobling but challenging insights of Jesus in the biblical Gospels, compare them with what is probably the most famous of the so-called gnostic gospels, the Gospel of Thomas, which came along more than a century later:

> Jesus is quoted in Saying 14 of Thomas as telling his disciples, "If you fast, you will bring sin upon yourselves, and if you pray, you will be condemned, and if you give to charity, you will harm your spirits." He is quoted in Saying 114 as teaching that "every female who makes herself male will enter the kingdom of Heaven." The gospel also quotes Jesus in Saying 7 as offering this inscrutable insight: "Blessings on the lion if a human

eats it, making the lion human. Foul is the human if a
lion eats it, making the lion human."[4]

Fasting leads to sin? Giving to charity damages your spirit? Women have to make themselves into men in order to get into heaven? (My female friends aren't going to like hearing this!) Lions who eat humans become humans themselves? Does any of that make sense to you? If your reaction is anything like mine, you're probably ready to get back to the real Jesus of history, as described in the genuine Gospels of Matthew, Mark, Luke, and John. I think it's apparent, because of their matchless clarity and consistency (not only with each other, but also with common sense about the world we live in), that the biblical Gospels, along with the other books of the Bible, have the earmarks of truth.

ARROW 7: THE BIBLE IS A UNIQUELY *HISTORICAL* RELIGIOUS BOOK.

The accounts in the Bible, particularly those in the New Testament, are based mostly on direct, eyewitness testimony. For example, the apostle John wrote, "That which was from the beginning, which we have heard, which we have seen with our eyes, which we have looked at and our hands have touched—this we proclaim."[5] Other parts of the New Testament were compiled by writers who interacted with various eyewitnesses. These writers include careful and conscientious historians like Luke, who made a point of explaining his research methodology: "Many people have set out to write accounts about the events that have been fulfilled among us. They used the eyewitness reports circulating among us from the early disciples. Having carefully investigated everything from the beginning, I also have decided to write a careful account . . . so you can be certain of the truth of everything you were taught."[6]

These accounts also were written down early—soon after the events they chronicle and easily within the lifespan of the people who walked with Jesus. I mention this because there are still some outdated rumors circulating that say the New Testament Gospels were penned at a much later time. One of the early proponents of that theory, theologian John A. T. Robinson, did additional research and made a dramatic turnaround. In fact, he later repudiated his previous claims and wrote a book titled *Redating the New Testament*, which corrected what he and others had been teaching.[7] In it, Robinson argues that the entire New Testament was written before AD 70. (To put this in context, the date of Jesus' resurrection is widely believed to have been in AD 30 or 33.) But even if the last part of the New Testament was written a bit later—say closer to AD 90, as many scholars believe, it's clear that the entire New Testament was completed within a generation of Christ's death and resurrection. That means there were many people still living who could vouch for its accuracy.

To put this in a modern perspective, most of the New Testament would have been completed within a span of years similar to the time that has elapsed since the assassination of John F. Kennedy (1963), the first visit of the Beatles to America (1964), and the first time a man walked on the moon (1969)—events that are vividly remembered by many of us today. And even the latest books would have been written within a span of years comparable to the time that has elapsed since the modern state of Israel was founded (1948), again well within the lifespan and memory of many people alive today. Obviously, if somebody now tried to rewrite history about any of those modern events, it would be quickly detected and refuted.[8] But we have no record of any contemporaries of the New Testament writers trying to factually challenge what had been written, which gives further confirmation that it was true.

The historical nature of the New Testament is also confirmed by a subsequent line of disciples who wrote and affirmed what had been taught from the beginning, including the early church fathers Polycarp, Ignatius, and Clement. Moreover, various details of the New Testament claims are reinforced by early outside reports, such as those by Thallus, Roman historians Tacitus and Suetonius, the Jewish historian Josephus, and others.[9]

It's also interesting to contrast the Bible to other religious writings, such as the Qur'an. Muslims generally grant that the Qur'an does not claim to be a historical book as much as a book of religious laws. Even so, it makes detailed claims about Jesus' life and teachings based on Muhammad's writings six hundred years later and six hundred miles from the scene. (As we saw in chapter 5, these claims are contradicted by eyewitness accounts written by people who were actually with Jesus and who wrote firsthand biographies about him.) We can also compare the Bible to the Book of Mormon, which is based on golden tablets that Joseph Smith allegedly dug up near his home in Manchester, New York, and translated into English before they were whisked away by an angel (these writings contain many claims that are not supported by either history or archaeology); or to Hindu writings, which largely don't make historical claims at all.[10] When you do these sorts of comparisons, the Bible really shines as a book with impressive historical credentials.

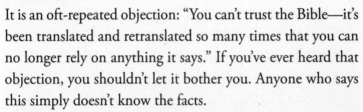

ARROW 8: THE BIBLE IS A UNIQUELY *PRESERVED* WORK OF ANTIQUITY.

It is an oft-repeated objection: "You can't trust the Bible—it's been translated and retranslated so many times that you can no longer rely on anything it says." If you've ever heard that objection, you shouldn't let it bother you. Anyone who says this simply doesn't know the facts.

The Bible we have today is not the end of some long chain of translations from one language to the next—say, from Greek to Latin, then Latin to German, then German to English, and so on. Rather, it is a direct translation from the historical manuscripts in the original languages—Hebrew for the Old Testament and Greek for the New Testament. Every good version goes back to the earliest documents and, based on many years of linguistic and cultural studies, puts what was written there into accurate contemporary language. The result is that we can easily read and understand what was originally recorded in Hebrew and Greek by the biblical writers.[11]

Also, for the New Testament, we have more than 5,800 copies of early Greek manuscripts or partial manuscripts[12]— and about 20,000 more in other languages.[13] As is the case with all ancient writings, we don't have the original hand-written documents themselves (called the *autographs*), but we do have an astounding number of reliable copies.

What makes the New Testament really stand out is that we have so many *more* copies than we have for any other ancient work, and they are so much *earlier* (in other words, dating closer to the time of the original writing). According to New Testament scholar Daniel B. Wallace, we have

> *an embarrassment of riches compared to the data the classical Greek and Latin scholars have to contend with. The average classical author's literary remains number no more than twenty copies. We have more than 1,000 times the manuscript data for the New Testament than we do for the average Greco-Roman author. Not only this, but the extant manuscripts of the average classical author are no earlier than 500 years after the time he wrote. For the New Testament, we are waiting mere decades for surviving copies.*[14]

These other historical works are still considered reliable. That being the case, when you consider the thousands of New Testament manuscripts and a "time gap" that is so amazingly small, there really is no question that the New Testament is historically reliable.

Also, because we have so many New Testament manuscripts, we can compare and study them to determine to an amazing degree of precision what the originals actually said. Some critics today, like Bart Ehrman, are trying to make the differences between these copies seem like a big problem. But the truth is that the differences are mostly insignificant, and none of them affects any important teachings or doctrines. Although it's true that having more copies makes for more variations between those copies, it's also true that we have a much greater opportunity to ascertain the original message accurately. Compare the New Testament to the writings of Plato, for example, of which we have only seven copies. When there's a variance among those seven copies, it's a much bigger guess to figure out which version to trust.

John Ankerberg described the situation on one of his television broadcasts: "Suppose we had a classroom of fifty high school seniors and we asked them to hand copy the Declaration of Independence. The A students would make very few errors; the B students perhaps a few more; the C students a fair number—and my friends would make a lot! But if we compared them all, we could easily reconstruct what the Declaration of Independence says."[15]

If that illustration has power with just fifty high school students of varying abilities and motivation levels, how much more does it show the overwhelming accuracy of more than five thousand manuscripts copied by people whose lives were all about the message they were seeking to preserve?

Sir Frederic Kenyon, British scholar and one-time director of the London Museum, summed it up well when he said, "The last foundation for any doubt that the Scriptures have come down to us substantially as they were written has now been removed. Both the authenticity and the general integrity of the books of the New Testament may be regarded as finally established."[16]

Similar evidence shows the integrity and reliability of the Old Testament text—including more recent discoveries of much earlier copies, such as those of Isaiah found in the

Dead Sea Scrolls, which show that the text has been preserved with remarkable accuracy.

The bottom line is that the modern translations of the Bible available to us today are accurate and trustworthy renditions of the original biblical texts—and we can read them with confidence.[17]

ARROW 9: ARCHAEOLOGY SHOWS THE BIBLE TO BE A POWERFULLY *VERIFIED* BOOK.

In an earlier chapter, I showed how one dispute—over the existence of the Hittite people described in the Old Testament—was clearly answered through archaeological research that strongly confirmed the Bible's assertion. This same pattern has been repeated literally thousands of times as various cities, nations, leaders, kings, languages, customs, and events mentioned in the Bible—many of which had previously been doubted by scholars—have been documented through the discovery and analysis of various artifacts.[18]

Sir William Ramsay, one of the great archaeologists of the late nineteenth and early twentieth centuries, started out as a staunch skeptic, doubting many details recorded in the New Testament. But then he spent thirty years of his life tracking down and confirming example after example of claims made in the Gospel of Luke, as well as in Luke's second work, the book of Acts. Here's what Ramsay finally conceded: "Luke is a historian of the first rank. . . . This author should be placed along with the very greatest of historians."[19]

Renowned archaeologist Nelson Glueck, who was once featured on the cover of *Time* magazine, said, "No archaeological discovery has ever controverted a single biblical reference. Scores of archaeological findings have been made which confirm in clear outline or exact detail historical statements in the Bible. And, by the same token, proper evaluation of biblical descriptions has often led to amazing discoveries."[20]

Another of the world's great archaeologists, William F. Albright, declared, "All radical schools in New Testament criticism which have existed in the past or which exist today are pre-archeological, and are therefore, since they were built in *der Luft* [in the air], quite antiquated today."[21]

The bottom line from an archaeological perspective: *don't bet against the Bible*. Time and again it has proven to be trustworthy in even its incidental details—which gives us confidence that its reporting of more important matters is equally accurate.

ARROW 10: THE BIBLE SHOWS ITSELF TO BE A UNIQUELY *HONEST* RELIGIOUS BOOK.

Some have argued over the years that Christianity is merely a matter of wish fulfillment. The theory is that people wanted a religion that would make them feel better, so they projected a heavenly Father into the sky and started pretending he actually existed.[22] Then they invented all kinds of other myths and stories about virgin births, miracles, and resurrections to go with it.

Here's a major problem with this theory—and a strong argument for the reliability of the scriptural record: the Bible contains a lot of sobering or unflattering information that in no way fits what people would make up if they were inventing a religion.

For example, sometimes the God of the Bible gets tired of

people's disobedience, so he brings punishment, not only on his enemies but sometimes even on his friends—and occasionally in ways that seem abrupt and harsh. This God declares that he will ultimately judge those who persist in their rebellion against him, allowing them to go their own way not only in this life, but eventually all the way into eternity—to a place of lasting separation and regret, called hell.

Now, you may not like everything the Bible teaches, but nobody would make these things up to soothe their minds or to try to make everyone feel better. These are not feel-good, fairy-tale concepts. The book of Proverbs says, "Faithful are the wounds of a friend; but the kisses of an enemy are deceitful."[23] The Bible sometimes conveys some very serious "wounds."

The Bible is also brutally honest about the ethical and moral failures of some of its key characters, including some of its own writers. This goes against the natural, built-in, human aversion to casting ourselves in a negative light—yet the writers of the Bible tell it how it really happened. Surely they wouldn't bring up these humiliating and often self-incriminating examples unless they were highly committed to reporting the real truth.

Even the core message of the Bible—that we all have corrupted hearts that lead us into moral failure and turn us into spiritually bankrupt people who desperately need to be rescued—is not the stuff of religious happy talk. I know it's not the script that *I* would have written.

These negative, but realistic, elements point to something positive—the Bible's reliability as a trustworthy historical record. This also undergirds the authenticity of its claim of being a book that communicates life-giving truth from God.

ARROW 11: *MIRACLES*, PERFORMED IN THE PRESENCE OF BELIEVERS AND CRITICS ALIKE, POINT TO THE PROPHETS, APOSTLES, AND JESUS AS MESSENGERS OF GOD.

Up to this point, I've largely argued that the Bible is a historically reliable book that has been tested and proven in a variety of ways. I'm confident that this is true and that the Bible will continue to withstand the attacks being leveled against it. But what gets interesting is that, as a credible historical record, the Bible reports events that are explainable only through supernatural means: events, for example, such as miracles. These included turning water into wine, walking on water, calming storms, multiplying a few fish and loaves of bread in order to feed thousands, healing people of a variety of diseases and physical handicaps, restoring sight to the blind—and the list goes on.

Now, some people immediately write off claims of the miraculous. When asked why, they'll simply say things like, "Miracles are impossible" or, "They would be breaking the laws of nature, and that can never happen."

Let me offer a few thoughts:

Many miracles are natural events timed in supernatural ways—thus, they do not break any laws of nature. An example would be the time when Jesus was in a boat during an intense storm, and he stretched out his hand to calm the wind and the waves. Now, a storm ending is nothing out of the ordinary—all storms eventually subside. But when it happens immediately upon Jesus' command, that's something miraculous.

It might also be good to rethink what a "law of nature" is. These "laws" are not inviolable principles, recorded in the sky somewhere, by which all natural things must forever abide— or else! Rather, they are generalizations or patterns based on observation; they're descriptive, not prescriptive. They talk about the way things normally happen, not the way they must happen. But if it was God who set things up to go the way they usually do, it should be no problem for him, the ultimate cause of the universe, to do something a bit different now and then. In fact, if he is a creative, powerful, and wise God, then stopping storms on cue, causing a virgin to bear a son, healing the sick, and even raising the dead would all be but mere child's play to him.

I would caution anyone who doubts whether miracles can really happen: don't make up your mind before you see the actual evidence. Otherwise, you'll be exhibiting classic, closed-minded prejudice (which literally means to "pre-judge"), which might preclude you from seeing or experiencing something authentically supernatural. Instead, find out what the witnesses actually saw, what made them think it was real, whether the other witnesses agreed on the essential details, how they tested it or thought about it critically, whether they're sticking with their story over the long haul, how the critics reacted and what kinds of evidence they brought against it, whether any of those critics changed their minds based on what they saw or learned, and so forth. Open your mind, investigate carefully, and let the evidence guide you to the truth about the matter.

One thing worth noting is that Jesus' miracles were not contested by his enemies. The miracles were too obviously real—so instead they would try to catch him on a technicality. "Sure, you healed the man," they would say, "but you did it on the Sabbath day, which is a big no-no."[24] But don't miss the fact that their accusations were inadvertent admissions that he'd done something miraculous. Otherwise, what were they accusing him of?

My advice to both Christians and skeptics is to read the biblical accounts for yourself, with your mind receptive to learning what actually happened, rather than being dead set against what you "*know* could not have happened." When you approach historical accounts with an open mind, I think you'll see some exciting new doors of discovery begin to open, along with a growing sense of confidence in what God can do.

ARROW 12: *FULFILLED PROPHECIES* POINT TO THE BIBLE AS A DIVINELY INSPIRED BOOK AND TO JESUS AS THE UNIQUE MESSIAH OF GOD.

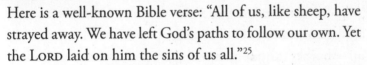

Here is a well-known Bible verse: "All of us, like sheep, have strayed away. We have left God's paths to follow our own. Yet the LORD laid on him the sins of us all."[25]

Dr. Michael Rydelnik tells the story of what a man he knows did with this passage:

> *I had a friend who typed this [Isaiah 53:6] up on his computer, but without any verse notations, and took it around to everyone in his office in the motor vehicle bureau in the state capital. He said, "Just tell me who this is and where it comes from."*
>
> *Every single person that looked at it, Jew or Gentile alike, read it and said, "It is obviously Jesus of Nazareth, that's who it is. And it is from the New Testament."*

And then my friend would say, "No, it is not from the New Testament. It is from the Hebrew Bible. It was written eight centuries before Jesus came. Can you believe this?" And he showed it to them from Isaiah, and people really had a hard time with it. Because if you read this passage without any kind of presuppositions or bias, it will be really clear that this is the life of Yeshua (Jesus).[26]

Biblical prophecy is amazing—and the deeper you look, the more astounding it becomes. For instance, if you read Isaiah 53 in its entirety, it will be clear that the entire chapter is an amazing prophecy of the suffering of the Messiah, yet it was written hundreds of years before the event. It describes, in advance, how Jesus was "pierced for our rebellion, crushed for our sins. He was beaten so we could be whole. He was whipped so we could be healed."[27]

Another prophecy says that people will look on the one "whom they have pierced and mourn for him as for an only son. They will grieve bitterly for him as for a firstborn son who has died."[28] It's easy to look at the crucifixion of Jesus from our side of history and clearly see how his brutal death fulfilled these prophetic words. But what really shows the divine insight in the words of these prophets is that these descriptions were written not only hundreds of years before the life and death of Christ, but also centuries before the Roman practice of crucifixion had even been invented (with its horrific piercing of the hands and feet with nails that were pounded into the wood of the cross). I imagine that the prophets who penned these words were scratching their heads in bewilderment as they sensed God leading them to write about how the suffering Messiah would be "pierced."

It's also interesting that Jesus, while hanging on the cross, called the attention of those standing nearby to the Old Testament passage of Psalm 22. He did this by quoting the first line of the psalm, crying out, "My God, my God, why have you forsaken me?"[29] This was a standard way in that culture for teachers to focus their listeners on a particular place in the Hebrew Scriptures.

But when you look at the rest of that psalm, you see that it also predicts numerous details concerning the suffering and sacrificial death of the Messiah. Here are a few of those phrases, including yet another ancient prediction about his being pierced, but adding the astonishing detail that the piercing would be through his hands and feet. Keep in mind that these words were penned about a thousand years before Jesus' crucifixion:

> *My God, my God, why have you forsaken me? Why are you so far from saving me, so far from the words of my groaning? . . . All who see me mock me; they hurl insults, shaking their heads: "He trusts in the LORD; let the LORD rescue him.". . . I am poured out like water, and all my bones are out of joint. My heart has turned to wax; it has melted away within me. My strength is dried up like a potsherd, and my tongue sticks to the roof of my mouth; you lay me in the dust of death. . . . A band of evil men has encircled me, they have pierced my hands and my feet. I can count all my bones; people*

*stare and gloat over me. They divide my garments
among them and cast lots for my clothing.*[30]

If you read about the Crucifixion as it is recorded in
the Gospels,[31] it is mind boggling how these centuries-old
predictions were fulfilled in such minute detail. Could any
mere human have written such specific history in advance?
It seems abundantly clear that God's foreknowledge was on
display in these predictions—and we've only mentioned a
few of the many examples that could be discussed. Others
include the place of the Messiah's birth being in Bethlehem,[32]
his being of the lineage of King David,[33] his being born of
a virgin,[34] his deity,[35] his being rejected by his own people,[36]
his betrayal for thirty pieces of silver,[37] his extreme suffering
and disfigurement,[38] his death on our behalf,[39] his burial in a
rich man's tomb,[40] and his subsequent resurrection.[41] Many
other examples could be listed, though these are some of the
most prominent.

Obviously, Jesus (if he were merely human) could not
manipulate circumstances in order to intentionally fulfill
these predictions. And the odds of these prophecies all being
fulfilled by one person are vanishingly small. "Someone did
the math and figured out that the probability of just eight
[messianic] prophecies being fulfilled is one chance in one
hundred million billion," said one Jewish man who found
Jesus as his Messiah. "That number is millions of times
greater than the total number of people who've ever walked
the planet."[42]

I won't trouble you with the number of zeros it would
take to represent the odds of forty-eight messianic prophecies

being fulfilled by one person. Just trust me when I tell you that the number is overwhelming.[43]

On resurrection Sunday, Jesus walked along a road with two of his followers who were trying to understand the events of his crucifixion. At first, they were prevented from recognizing him as he admonished them with these words: "You foolish people! You find it so hard to believe all that the prophets wrote in the Scriptures. Wasn't it clearly predicted that the Messiah would have to suffer all these things before entering his glory?"[44] Then Jesus explained to these men everything the Hebrew Scriptures had predicted about him.

It wasn't until a bit later, just after he had left them, that the travelers realized it had actually been Jesus. In awe they said to each other, "Didn't our hearts burn within us as he talked with us on the road and explained the Scriptures to us?"[45]

For me, these prophecies, along with the accounts of miracles and the other arguments we discussed in this chapter, serve as further reasons to trust the Bible—not only as an accurate historical record, but also as one that is divinely inspired and therefore uniquely suited to guide us into a confident faith. More than that, they serve as further evidence in the cumulative case for the validity of Christianity.

CHAPTER TWELVE

HOW HISTORY AND EXPERIENCE POINT TOWARD SPIRITUAL TRUTH

The doors were locked; but suddenly, as before, Jesus was standing among them. "Peace be with you," he said. Then he said to Thomas, "Put your finger here, and look at my hands. Put your hand into the wound in my side. Don't be faithless any longer. Believe!"
"My Lord and my God!" Thomas exclaimed.
Then Jesus told him, "You believe because you have seen me. Blessed are those who believe without seeing me."

JOHN 20:26-29

In this chapter, we'll explore the historical and experiential realms, looking at a number of additional "arrows" in the broader arsenal of information that point to not only the existence of God, but also the truth of the Christian faith.

ARROW 13: JESUS' *SINLESS LIFE* BACKED UP HIS CLAIM TO BE THE SON OF GOD.

In an age when so many religious leaders talk a good game but fail to live up to their own press releases, it's a huge relief to find out that nobody was able to show that Jesus had committed any kind of sin or wrongdoing—*ever*. That included his closest companions, as well as the critical Pharisees—who followed him around looking for any kind of character flaw, hint of moral or ethical inconsistency, or even old-fashioned human mistakes and frailty. But nothing was reported in terms of defects or weaknesses—not even from Jesus' own mother, who certainly would have known!

This is important—not because a leader needs to be perfect in order to be followed, but because Jesus claimed repeatedly to be the Son of God. If that claim was true, it would certainly require that he be sinless and without flaw.

Throughout the four Gospels, we frequently see Jesus' enemies trying to catch him doing something—anything—wrong. But they were always left quibbling over peripheral details, like whether Jesus kept certain obscure rules to the letter of the law.[1] And in the end, these opponents were the ones who had to pay false witnesses to invent and tell stories in order to try to accuse Jesus of wrongdoing. Knowing as they did that none of it was true, you can imagine their frustration when at one point Jesus even threw the reality of his sinless life back in their faces. "Which of you can truthfully accuse me of sin?" he asked them.[2]

When it was all said and done, the only accusation that they could make stick against Jesus was that of blasphemy—for which they ended up indicting him because "he called God his Father, thereby making himself equal with God."[3] His claim to equality with the Father *would* have been blasphemy—had it not been true.

By contrast, I know of no other major religious leaders who claimed to be sinless. Muhammad, for example, was very open about his need for God's forgiveness. In the Qur'an he says he was told to "patiently, then, persevere: for the Promise of Allah is true: and *ask forgiveness for thy fault*, and celebrate the Praises of thy Lord in the evening and in the morning."[4]

Joseph Smith Jr., the founder of Mormonism, died in a gun battle in which he defended himself with a six-shooter; a later Mormon president who was at the scene said that Smith even killed two people in the fight. While many Mormons liken this event to the prophetic passage in Isaiah 53, saying Smith was "led like a lamb to the slaughter," the comparison of Smith with Jesus is really a study in contrasts. Jesus willingly laid down his life for his friends, and he did nothing to defend himself against his accusers.

Jesus stands alone as a leader you can respect, imitate, trust, and follow in *everything*—without fear of embarrassment or recrimination. His words and actions, without exception, back up his claim to being the unique Son of God and give us confidence that he is worthy of our faith and obedience.

ARROW 14: JESUS' *RESURRECTION* POWERFULLY ESTABLISHED HIS CREDENTIALS AS THE SON OF GOD.

Three days after his crucifixion, Jesus miraculously rose from the dead, just as he'd predicted.[5] This supernatural event has been well documented and attested to in a number of compelling ways. I'll briefly discuss three of those ways here, though the next few "arrows" further support the historic reality of the resurrection.

Jesus' tomb was empty.

Starting with the women who first visited the tomb and then the men who followed soon after, the disciples all testified that it was empty—in bewilderment at first because they didn't fully grasp what had happened. But nobody, not even the disciples' enemies, disputed the fact that the tomb was vacant. Instead, the religious authorities made up a story and bribed the guards, coaching them to say, "Jesus' disciples came during the night while we were sleeping, and they stole his body."[6] If you reflect on this statement for just a moment, you'll realize how ridiculous their story was. If the guards had really been asleep, they wouldn't have had any idea what happened to the body. On the other hand, if they had seen the disciples stealing the body, they would have stopped and arrested them. But their fabricated story *does* do something useful: it concedes that the tomb really was empty, and it demonstrates that the religious leaders had no idea how to explain it.

Let me also note that there's no good rationale for saying that anyone stole or moved the body. The *Romans*, who were ruling in Palestine at the time, wanted Jesus dead, and they crucified him. They had no interest or motivation to do anything that would make anyone think otherwise. The *Jewish leaders* wanted Jesus dead (and they wanted him to *stay* dead). If there had been a body to be found, you can bet they would have put it on display to quash the upstart movement of Christianity that was threatening their authority. The *disciples* were scared to death after the Crucifixion, and they—including Peter, who was grief stricken and full of shame after repeatedly denying Jesus during his trial—were hiding in a room and trying to decide what to do next. The disciples had neither the motivation nor the means to overcome the guards, steal Jesus' body, and then—what?—make up stories and lie about it for the rest of their lives, face persecution, and end up becoming martyrs for no good reason? I don't think so! The best explanation for Jesus' empty tomb is Jesus' resurrection.

The risen Jesus was seen by eyewitnesses.

With the possible exception of John, the early disciples did not believe in Jesus' resurrection merely because of the empty tomb—they believed in it because they saw the risen Jesus, talked to him, and even ate with him. Two leading authorities on the Resurrection, Gary Habermas and Michael Licona, write in *The Case for the Resurrection of Jesus* that "friends as well as foes saw Jesus not once but many times over a period of forty days. We are told that these numbers included both men and women, hard-hearted Peter and softhearted Mary Magdalene, indoors and outdoors."[7]

And let's not forget the doubting disciple named Thomas. Maybe you can relate to him. Thomas wouldn't believe in any resurrection claims without solid evidence. But then he met the risen Jesus and saw the scars on his hands and side. Convinced, Thomas humbly exclaimed, "My Lord and my God!"[8]—which is the appropriate response, once you understand who Jesus is and what he has done for us.

The accounts of the risen Jesus were frequent and early.

After the followers of Jesus realized what had happened—that he truly had conquered the grave—they immediately started telling people about it. Their reports were oral at first but were soon written down as well.

One of the earliest creeds of the church, which scholars believe originated within, at most, just a few years of Jesus' resurrection, is recorded by Paul:

> *I passed on to you what was most important and what had also been passed on to me. Christ died for our sins, just as the Scriptures said. He was buried, and he was raised from the dead on the third day, just as the Scriptures said. He was seen by Peter and then by the Twelve. After that, he was seen by more than 500 of his followers at one time, most of whom are still alive, though some have died. Then he was seen by James and later by all the apostles. Last of all . . . I also saw him.*[9]

This testimony, along with corroborating accounts in the four Gospels and other books of the New Testament, simply affirms what was well known to Christians ever since the first Easter Sunday—and it leaves no doubt regarding the clarity these early Christ-followers had about the reality of the Resurrection. Their confidence, along with the reasons that persuaded them, assures us of the bedrock reality of the resurrection of Jesus—and, with it, the truthfulness of his claim to be the Son of God.

ARROW 15: THE *EMERGENCE OF THE CHURCH* POINTS TO THE AUTHENTICITY OF ITS MESSAGE.

It truly was an incredible turn of events. Peter had assured Jesus that he would follow him even to death, but then he denied Jesus three times that very same night. After Jesus was tortured and crucified, the defeated Peter went in fear and trembling to hide out in some first-century safe house, along with the rest of the ragtag band of dejected disciples.

Fast forward only a few weeks. Now Peter and the others are out in the public square—in Jerusalem, the very city where

Jesus had been crucified less than two months earlier—and they are boldly telling anyone who will listen about the risen Christ. And if that's not enough, Peter then storms the stage and begins to preach to this potentially hostile crowd:

> *People of Israel, listen! God publicly endorsed Jesus the Nazarene by doing powerful miracles, wonders, and signs through him, as you well know. But God knew what would happen, and his prearranged plan was carried out when Jesus was betrayed. With the help of lawless Gentiles, you nailed him to a cross and killed him. But God released him from the horrors of death and raised him back to life, for death could not keep him in its grip. . . .*
>
> *God raised Jesus from the dead, and we are all witnesses of this. Now he is exalted to the place of highest honor in heaven, at God's right hand. . . .*
>
> *So let everyone in Israel know for certain that God has made this Jesus, whom you crucified, to be both Lord and Messiah!*[10]

The crowd's response? If Jesus had not risen from the dead, then Peter and his companions would have been—at best—laughed out of town! The Roman or Jewish leaders could have easily quashed this entire movement by pulling the body of Jesus back out of the tomb, throwing it in a wheelbarrow, and parading it up and down Main Street.

"Here's your dead Messiah," they could have taunted, adding, "Is this really the guy you want us to follow?"—with devastating effect.

No, the emergence of the church was too tied to claims of the resurrection of Jesus to have been possible without that resurrection really happening. This is not like the rise of Islam or Buddhism or many other religions that are linked to a general set of teachings, rather than to a miraculous make-or-break historical event.

In light of that, how did the crowd react to Peter's bold claims? The record tells us his words "pierced their hearts," and they cried out and asked what they should do. Peter instructed them to "repent of your sins and turn to God, and be baptized in the name of Jesus Christ for the forgiveness of your sins."[11] And guess what? About three thousand people did just that. And this was only the beginning of the rapid emergence and exponential growth of the Christian church. This growth has continued to this day, with Christianity becoming the largest religion in the world, now with more adherents in the developing world than in the entire Western world combined.[12]

Again, this would never have happened if Peter had not been telling the truth when he so boldly proclaimed his message about Jesus. And let's not overlook that he backed up his assertions with phrases like "as you well know" and "we are all witnesses to this." This appeal to public knowledge was also used by Paul when he unflinchingly declared during one of his speeches, "King Agrippa knows about these things. I speak boldly, for I am sure these events are all familiar to him, for they were not done in a corner!"[13]

These events confirm that the resurrection of Jesus really did happen; the early church was confident about it as an established fact—as well as about their entire message and mission—and they were willing to stake everything on it (as we'll see in more detail in Arrow 17). That kind of confidence has proven to be spiritually contagious to millions of people ever since then, myself included.

ARROW 16: THE *CHANGED LIVES OF EARLY SKEPTICS* AFFIRMED THE TRUTH OF JESUS' RESURRECTION AND THE TEACHINGS OF THE CHURCH.

It's one thing that the friends and companions of Jesus stayed faithful to his teachings and endured against the odds. But when some who opposed the Christian movement—like Saul of Tarsus, who was an active persecutor of the church, and others who were skeptical of Jesus, like his own half brother James—ended up becoming Jesus' devoted disciples, well, that really said something.

Saul had been present and enthusiastically supportive of the condemnation and subsequent stoning of Stephen, a Christian disciple. The book of Acts records Stephen's valiant final speech, followed by his violent end as the first recorded martyr for Christ.[14] It also mentions specifically that "Saul was one of the witnesses, and he agreed completely with the killing of Stephen," and that he "was uttering threats with every breath and was eager to kill the Lord's followers."[15]

Saul was soon on his way to Damascus to drag any Christians he might find there back to Jerusalem. It was on that journey that the risen Jesus appeared to him, temporarily blinded him, and called him to become his follower and eventually a leader in the worldwide Christian movement.[16]

Saul, whom we know much better by his postconversion name of Paul the apostle, became a powerful proponent of the faith, developing into the world's most influential leader in the spread of the message of Jesus. He helped countless people find faith in Christ, and then he established churches in each city around those freshly committed believers.

Less was written about James, but he was evidently a doubter of the claims of his half brother, Jesus, as they grew up together. Later, however, he was one of the people Jesus visited after his resurrection,[17] and he ended up becoming a key leader in the early church.

Maybe you're thinking, *So these guys converted. Tom Cruise converted to Scientology. Madonna converted to Kaballah. That doesn't prove they're right.*

That's true. But there's a big difference between those kinds of examples and the change of mind that Paul and James experienced. First, Paul and James were there, living during Jesus' earthly ministry. They experienced many of the things we can only read about today. James grew up with Jesus and saw the way he lived, the miracles he performed, and the horrendous crucifixion he endured. Then, when all hope seemed lost, he met the risen Jesus—and for him that changed everything.[18]

Paul lived through these times as well, not as a follower of Jesus, but as one who could verify the reports of things he said and did. More than that, Paul, a passionately committed opponent of the Christian faith, was appeared to by the resurrected Savior.[19] This miraculous event turned him instantly from foe to friend. As a result, Paul became the greatest missionary the world has ever seen. In light of who he was and how strongly he had opposed Christianity, his turnaround was hugely significant—both then and now.

The closest equivalent I can think of today would be if suddenly the anti-God evolutionist Richard Dawkins, author of *The God Delusion*, announced that Jesus had appeared to him and convinced him he was going the wrong way—and that as a result he was denouncing his former positions, taking his book completely out of print, and giving his life to travel the world and spread the gospel. That would be a powerful testimony, though still not as persuasive as those of James and Paul, because Dawkins lives two millennia after the events surrounding Jesus' ministry.

Indeed, these two skeptics-turned-star-witnesses serve notice to the world—and to us as we consider the Christian truth claims—that this faith is built on a solid foundation of facts.

ARROW 17: THE *WILLINGNESS OF THE DISCIPLES TO DIE* FOR CLAIMS THEY KNEW TO BE TRUE AFFIRMS THE TRUSTWORTHINESS OF THEIR CLAIMS.

We left out a very important fact about the two former skeptics we just discussed: they not only made complete turn-arounds in their lives to become followers of Jesus, but they also were willing to die for the truth of their claims. This shows the level of their confidence in what they had seen and experienced, especially as witnesses of the risen Jesus.

Equally significant is the fact that almost all the other disciples—who said they saw, talked to, and ate with the risen Jesus, some of them multiple times—also died willingly as martyrs for the truth of those claims. They all refused to deny or diminish anything they had proclaimed about Jesus, his miracles, his teachings, or his resurrection.

It's fairly easy to embrace the Christian faith today, especially in the Western culture of freedom and tolerance. But the disciples' willingness to proclaim it in their time and culture, and eventually to die for it, provides a huge exclamation point to the fact that they really believed what they so boldly proclaimed.

Some people have tried to discredit the importance of this argument by equating the disciples, and their willingness to lay down their lives, with members of other religions who have voluntarily died for their faith. The most common comparison is to modern Muslim terrorists, such as the ones who gave up their lives to fly airplanes into the World Trade Center and the Pentagon on September 11, 2001. The rationale is that they, too, were willing to die for what they believed.

However, there is a major difference between these two examples: the disciples of Jesus had been in a position *to know for certain* whether or not what they claimed was correct. They were either telling the truth about being with the risen Savior or they were lying—but either way they knew what had really happened. So if Jesus did not rise from the dead, they knew they were lying about seeing him, and they went ahead and gave their lives for that lie anyway.

Who would do that? Who would say to themselves and to each other, "We know this resurrection story didn't really happen; we know we're going to have to lie about it for the rest of our lives—acting in complete disobedience to everything Jesus taught us about telling the truth; we know we're going to be persecuted and probably die for this lie; we know we've got nothing to gain and everything to lose; we know we'll never be able to respect ourselves or look each other in the eye again;

we know that the religion we're inventing will be a complete sham; we know we'll be judged eventually by God for all of this; and we know we don't have to do any of this.

"But we're going to get our stories together (more or less) anyway, and tell them to the ends of the earth. We're all going to give the same false report—all the way to prison and to death, as we stand united for this manufactured myth. Is everybody in?"

Can you imagine it? I certainly can't. What would have been the upside? The real truth is this: *nobody dies for what they* know *to be a lie.*

Instead, the disciples' eventual deaths, which were the direct result of resolutely holding to their claims to have seen the resurrected Jesus, speak *volumes* about the truthfulness of those claims. And if they were willing to die for what they knew, we ought to take it very seriously.

The Muslim terrorists, on the other hand, were not in a position to know anything for certain. Yes, they had been *taught* that their impending crimes were Allah's will and that their deaths would ensure their immediate entry into paradise, but there was no way for them to verify those teachings. So those men yielded to the authority of their extremist teachers, took a blind leap of faith, and gave up their lives for what they could only hope against hope—and against reason and conscience—was really God's will.

Because they had no way of proving ahead of time the reality of what they'd been promised, neither their deaths nor those of any others in this state of blind submission do anything to prove the truthfulness of their religion.

See the difference? The claims of Christianity are bolstered by the sacrifices and deaths of those who were there at the beginning and who knew for certain whether it all happened the way they said it did. Their certitude, along with their willingness to give up everything to remain faithful to what they had seen and heard, should give us great confidence in these things as well.

ARROW 18: THE *CHANGED MINDS OF MANY MODERN SKEPTICS* FURTHER SUPPORT THE CHRISTIAN TRUTH CLAIMS.

This argument represents a different kind of reason for believing than the turnarounds of the early skeptics. Their change of mind points primarily to the validity of their experience with the risen Christ. However, the conversions of modern skeptics points more to the strength of the evidence (including the "arrows" in this book) still available to all of us today. Here are a few of many examples we could talk about:

Simon Greenleaf was a Jewish scholar and one of two professors who built Harvard Law School into the world-class institution it is today. He also wrote the standard textbook on what constitutes good arguments in a court of law: the three-volume *Treatise on the Law of Evidence*. So brilliant was this work that the *London Law Magazine* once declared that through it "more light has shone from the New World than from all the lawyers who adorn the courts of Europe."[20] Professor Greenleaf was challenged one day by some of his students to examine the evidence for the resurrection of Christ. Skeptical at first, he thoroughly investigated that evidence and ended up becoming an ardent follower of Jesus. He later wrote a defense of the Christian faith called *The Testimony of the Evangelists: The Gospels Examined by the Rules of Evidence*.

A. H. Ross, an English journalist who set out to publish a popular book exposing the myth of the resurrection of Christ, ended up writing a book he had not intended. Using the pen name "Frank Morison," Ross initially titled his work *The Book That Refused to be Written*, but later changed it to *Who Moved the Stone?* As the name of this now-classic book indicates, Ross's studies convinced him—initially against his will—that Jesus really did rise from the dead. Once he was confident of that truth, Ross chose the Christian faith as his own and began telling others what he had discovered.

Sir Lionel Luckhoo was listed in the 1990 *Guinness Book of World Records* as the world's most successful lawyer. His amazing record as a defense attorney was 245 successive murder acquittals, either before a jury or on appeal. This brilliant barrister, twice knighted by Queen Elizabeth, rigorously analyzed the evidence for the resurrection of Jesus for several years before coming to the following conclusion: "I say unequivocally that the evidence for the Resurrection of Jesus Christ is so overwhelming that it compels acceptance by proof which leaves absolutely no room for doubt."[21]

Countless other stories could be told, including that of Josh McDowell, who as a college student set out to disprove Christianity and ended up becoming a believer. McDowell wrote *More Than a Carpenter*, a powerful little book about the evidence for Christ that has now sold more than fifteen million copies, and the encyclopedic *Evidence That Demands a Verdict*, which presents further evidence for the truth of Christianity.[22] Then there's the story of Viggo Olsen, who, as a medical student with a promising future as a surgeon, took a challenge from his wife's parents to examine the evidence for Christianity. What he thought would be a brief investigation turned into a life-changing spiritual quest. In the end, both Viggo and his wife, Joan, came to faith in Jesus. They subsequently spent thirty-three years as medical missionaries to the poor in Bangladesh.[23] And then there's my close friend and ministry partner, Lee Strobel, who as the skeptical legal editor for the *Chicago Tribune* investigated Christianity for nearly two years before finding faith in the risen Jesus. Today, Lee speaks and writes about the kinds of evidence that convinced him, which he describes in his bestsellers *The Case for Christ, The Case for Faith, The Case for a Creator, The Case for the Real Jesus,* and *The Case for Grace.*

The fact that so many smart people have carefully investigated the facts and ended up choosing the Christian faith doesn't necessarily make it true—but it certainly lends weight to that possibility. At a minimum, it seems it should motivate any sincere seeker to consider the points of evidence that have convinced so many other serious thinkers. And for those of us who are already Christians, it's yet one more reason for confidence in what we believe.

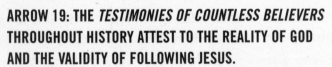

ARROW 19: THE *TESTIMONIES OF COUNTLESS BELIEVERS* THROUGHOUT HISTORY ATTEST TO THE REALITY OF GOD AND THE VALIDITY OF FOLLOWING JESUS.

In addition to the logical reasons and various points of evidence we've discussed, consider the fact that countless people, from extremely diverse backgrounds, cultures, and walks of life—all along the corridors of time—have found that faith in Jesus makes a significant difference in their daily lives as well as in their outlook for the future.

Yes, I know that lots of people believe lots of religious ideas—and that this alone doesn't prove that Christianity is true. Acknowledged. But when you've seen life after life dramatically changed through meeting Christ, when you've seen marriages saved and families mended, when you've seen self-centered people become others-centered and willing to self-sacrificially serve those less fortunate, when you've seen stingy people become generous, and when you realize these examples can be multiplied millions of times over, it all begins to accrue into a knowledge that God is alive and Jesus really does change lives for the better.

I certainly know that my life is improved because of God's guidance and wisdom, even if applied imperfectly. Over and over, God's ways, as revealed in the Bible, have shown themselves true. When I've carefully sought God's will and direction, they have consistently proven to be what's best for me. This is the case not only in the spiritual realm, but also in the relational, marital, and vocational areas of my life.

For me, placing my faith in Jesus has proven to be the best way to live—and I'm confident that someday it will also prove to be the best way to die.

ARROW 20: IT'S TRUE BECAUSE *JESUS SAID SO*—AND HE HAS THE CREDENTIALS TO SPEAK WITH AUTHORITY.

Have you ever noticed that almost everyone tries to claim Jesus, in one way or another, as their very own?

To the New Ager, he's an enlightened spiritual master; to the Baha'i or Muslim, he's a great prophet; to the liberal, he's another liberal; to the extreme fundamentalist, he's an angry street preacher; to the Unitarian, he's a universalist; to the corporate executive, he's the consummate business leader; to the Communist, he's the head of a commune; to the motivational teacher, he's the ultimate positive thinker; to postmodernists, he's many different things; and to the irreverent coworker, he's simply "the guy upstairs."

To our natural way of thinking, Jesus is everybody's buddy—and in almost every case, our image of him ends up looking suspiciously like ourselves. Someone quipped, "In the beginning, God created human beings in his own image—and we quickly returned him the favor." It's strange how one side of our brains desperately longs for a God who is transcendently exalted, and then the other side of our brains does everything it can to try to pull him down to our own mundane level.

In spite of all of this, I'd like to make a modest proposal: *Why don't we let Jesus speak for himself?* After all, he has credentials and credibility like nobody else. Of all the people who have walked this planet, he was the best at saying what he wanted to convey—sometimes with challenging words and often with encouraging ones.

Here are some of his challenging words that we'd be wise to pay heed to:

> *I am the way, the truth, and the life. No one can come to the Father except through me.*[24]

> *You will know the truth, and the truth will set you free.*[25]

And here are some of his encouraging words:

*Come to me, all of you who are weary and carry heavy
burdens, and I will give you rest. Take my yoke upon
you. Let me teach you, because I am humble and gentle
at heart, and you will find rest for your souls. For my
yoke is easy to bear, and the burden I give you is light.*[26]

We've now examined the Twenty Arrows of Truth. Let
me conclude this three-chapter section of reasons for the
Christian faith with a wise word of admonition from Simon
Greenleaf, the distinguished Harvard lawyer I mentioned
earlier:

*In examining the evidences of the Christian religion,
it is essential to the discovery of truth that we bring to
the investigation a mind freed, as far as possible, from
existing prejudice, and open to conviction. There should
be a readiness, on our part, to investigate with candor,
to follow the truth wherever it may lead us, and to
submit, without reserve or objection, to all the teachings
of this religion, if it be found to be of divine origin.*[27]

TEN BARRIERS TO BELIEF

How You Can Overcome the Impediments
That Block Your Faith

CHAPTER THIRTEEN

BREAKING THROUGH THE BARRIERS TO CONFIDENT FAITH

Truth is so obscure in these times, and falsehood so established,
that unless we love the truth, we cannot know it.

BLAISE PASCAL

I went mountain biking today. The weather was ideal: sunshine with a cool breeze. The trail twists through the woods near our home. The scenery is stunning, with views of the foothills nearby and the higher snowcapped peaks off in the distance. I often see deer and scare up a variety of other interesting animals. I love the scent of the pines and other fragrant trees, bushes, and wildflowers as I go pedaling by them.

I'm sorry to intrude on that idyllic image, but I should also mention that people sometimes get injured while biking the trails. There are plenty of boulders, washouts, and drop-offs that can send a rider suddenly airborne. Mechanical failure of the bike can also cause catastrophic crashes, like the one I heard about not long ago when the rider's handlebars collapsed as he landed from a jump. There are also poisonous insects and reptiles, as a friend of mine can attest—he was bitten by a rattlesnake.

And then there are the mountain lions.

I thought that they were sort of a joke when I first started riding—until I heard about a mountain biker who was actually killed by one. In fact, later that same day, a woman was mauled by the same angry cougar.

I once figured that because I ride fairly fast I was probably safe. But I did some research and learned that these cats—which can weigh up to 170 pounds and measure 8 feet long from nose to tail—can run 40 miles per hour, jump 20 feet straight into the air and up into a tree, and apparently are attracted to quick-moving prey, just as kittens are drawn to rolling balls of yarn.

Now I carry a knife and a cell phone whenever I ride (the state doesn't allow sawed-off shotguns), neither of which would probably help me, but at least I feel as if I've taken *some* precaution. It's not as if you can go out and buy mountain lion repellent.

The bottom line is this: to at least some degree, I ride by faith. I don't *know* that I'm going to be safe or come home in one piece, but the evidence and the odds weigh in my favor. In fact, statistically (in case you were wondering) it's about as unlikely to get killed by a mountain lion as it is to die of a shark attack—and the chances of either one are about 1/100 of the likelihood of being killed by lightning and 1/50,000 of the chance of dying in an automobile accident.[1] So if you ever go outside where you could possibly be struck by lightning—or, worse yet, if you're crazy enough to ever ride in a car—then you live by faith much more than I do when I'm out riding my mountain bike.

That's just the way life is. We pursue our normal, daily activities trusting that they'll work out more or less for the best—as they did yesterday, and the day before. There's no guarantee that this will actually be the case, but we work from the information we have and live our lives anyway.

CONFIDENT FAITH

Wise, spiritual faith—the kind I'm advocating—is a commitment of trust based on solid, though incomplete, evidence that we're believing in the right things and moving in the best direction. This understanding of faith, I should point out, is in sharp contrast to the fuzzy and often misguided definitions we see floating about in contemporary culture. Here are a few examples of those:

- *Wishful thinking*, in the relativistic, it's-true-for-you sense, which we discussed in chapter 3 and found lacking.

- *Therapeutic faith*, which is similar to wishful thinking, but based more on comfort and emotional positivity. In reality it may make you feel good but still be false.

- *Unfounded belief*, also known as *blind faith*, as described by atheist Richard Dawkins: "Faith is the great cop-out, the great excuse to evade the need to think and evaluate evidence. Faith is belief in spite of, even perhaps because of, the lack of evidence. . . . Faith is not allowed to justify itself by argument."[2] My friend Erick Nelson calls this approach to faith "a kind of voluntary, self-imposed frontal lobotomy"—which certainly neither he nor I would recommend.

- *Irrational faith*, an approach summed up in the classic example of the Sunday school kid who defined faith by saying, "It's believing in something even though you know in your heart it couldn't possibly be true."

Contrasted to all of that, I'm advocating what we've been calling *confident faith*—which is belief and action based on good logic and evidence, trustworthy revelation, and sometimes substantiated intuition, credentialed authority, and tested tradition. Confident faith moves in the same direction indicated by the facts, though it's a commitment or step that takes you further than the evidence alone can carry you.

Coming back to my example of mountain biking, I go out to ride when it seems safe, the bicycle is in good repair, the weather is good, and the trail looks inviting. I think I'll come back in one piece, but it still takes some faith (though only a little) to get on the bike. This faith is *action based on good evidence*.

Likewise, I believe in aviation. I accept what I understand about the science of flight. But just acknowledging those facts won't get me from Denver to Orange County when I need to go there this weekend. I'll need to move beyond *agreeing* with the information and actually *exercise enough faith* (a moderate amount) to climb on board the airplane and fly to Southern California.

I support the idea of marriage. I think the singular commitment of a man and a woman to one another for life is good for them, for their children, and for society in general. But that belief alone doesn't make me a husband. I still had to court the girl, pop the question, stand in front of the church, and say "I do." (That one took *lots* of faith—on *Heidi's* part!) And I still have to get up every morning and live out that commitment.

In each of these examples, faith entails two components: *right belief* (the bike is sound, the airplane will fly, the girl and I were made for each other) and *appropriate action* (I'll ride that bike, fly in that airplane, marry that girl). But how do those components—right belief and appropriate action— apply to the task of finding and enjoying a confident faith?

Well, you can review the previous three chapters for my understanding of the right belief part. In them, I laid out twenty reasons for trusting not only in a powerful and wise deity but, more specifically, in the teachings of Christianity. Many more arguments could be offered, but I'm optimistic that the ones I've presented are solid and will point you—and the family and friends you share them with—toward truth. For a quick review, here are the twenty reasons, or arrows, that I identified:

Arrow 1 → Design in the universe points to an *intelligent designer*.

Arrow 2 → Fine-tuning in the universe points to an intentional *fine-tuner*.

Arrow 3 → Information encoded into DNA points to a *divine encoder*.

Arrow 4 → The beginning of the universe points to a *divine originator*.

Arrow 5 → The sense of morality throughout the human race points to a *moral lawgiver*.

Arrow 6 → The Bible shows itself to be a uniquely *consistent* religious book.

Arrow 7 → The Bible is a uniquely *historical* religious book.

Arrow 8 → The Bible is a uniquely *preserved* work of antiquity.

Arrow 9 → Archaeology shows the Bible to be a powerfully *verified* book.

Arrow 10 → The Bible shows itself to be a uniquely *honest* religious book.

Arrow 11 → *Miracles*, performed in the presence of believers and critics alike, point to the prophets, apostles, and Jesus as messengers of God.

Arrow 12 → *Fulfilled prophecies* point to the Bible as a divinely inspired book and to Jesus as the unique Messiah of God.

Arrow 13 → Jesus' *sinless life* backed up his claim to be the Son of God.

Arrow 14 → Jesus' *resurrection* powerfully established his credentials as the Son of God.

Arrow 15 → The *emergence of the church* points to the authenticity of its message.

Arrow 16 → The *changed lives of early skeptics* affirmed the truth of Jesus' resurrection and the teachings of the church.

Arrow 17 → The *willingness of the disciples to die* for claims they knew to be true affirms the trustworthiness of their claims.

Arrow 18 → The *changed minds of many modern skeptics* further support the Christian truth claims.

Arrow 19 → The *testimonies of countless believers* throughout history attest to the reality of God and the validity of following Jesus.

Arrow 20 → It's true because *Jesus said so*—and he has the credentials to speak with authority.

Before I move on from the *right belief* component of faith, let me explain why I've described these reasons as *arrows*: it's because each one points toward a truth or set of truths, and away from all opposing viewpoints. Individually and collectively, they present information that takes you in a particular direction.

Here's a picture portraying this with the arrows representing the various arguments:

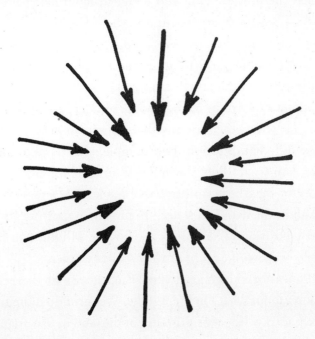

Now, as I mentioned, much more could be said and many more arrows added, though not every one will be equally persuasive to every individual. But the cumulative case—what lawyers call the preponderance of evidence—presents an awfully compelling set of arguments for the truth being in the center of that illustration. I'm not claiming we have absolute proof; no faith choice ever does. But from my study and observation, there is no other belief system that comes even close to the collective pattern of reasons and evidence we see in this diagram.

So again, whatever the truth is, it seems clear that it must fall somewhere in the middle of the picture. But what, specifically, is in the middle? When you look at all of the arguments presented, it's clear they point to *the one true God* who created the universe and who designed us in his image, to *Jesus as God's incarnate Son*, and to the Bible (both Old and New Testaments) as *God's revelation.*

Anyone who wants to argue for a completely different position has a difficult dual task: (1) to refute the reasons pointing to the truths in the middle of the chart, and (2) to come up with other reasons that point compellingly in a whole different direction. For example, atheists need to do more than try to shoot down the arguments for God's existence; for their belief to rise above the level of a mere "leap of faith in the dark," they need to present arguments *for* the atheist position. The same goes for the Hindu, Muslim, Baha'i, or New Age point of view—or any other.

But it's not enough just to know and agree with these conclusions about what's in the middle. We must do more than merely acknowledge the existence of the God of Christianity, nodding our heads in agreement to a list of biblical teachings. We must also respond to that God and what he has said. It was Jesus who asked his listeners, "Why do you keep calling me 'Lord, Lord!' when you don't do what I say?"[3] Faith is both right belief *and* appropriate action—moving in the direction that the evidence points.

So what is that *appropriate action*? Ultimately we must understand and respond to God's central message in the Bible, the gospel. This amazing message tells us that God loves us, but also that we have disobeyed and dishonored him, thus breaking off our relationship with him. Therefore we need his rescue and reclamation. That may be hard for you (or the friends you share it with) to hear, but there's an exciting upside: God chose to rescue us through Jesus, who came to earth not only to teach us and show us how to live but also to pay the penalty for our failure to live the way we should.

You see, our disobedience to God (what the Bible calls sin) resulted in our owing a serious moral debt, a spiritual death penalty that each of us has earned but can never fully pay—in this life or the next. On our own, we are helpless to do anything about it.

But God doesn't want to leave us in this hopeless predicament. He cares too much about us not to provide us with a way of escape. So he came to earth in the person of Jesus, and at the appointed time, allowed him to be accused, tried, and executed—not because he had done anything wrong, but because *we* had.

Jesus summed up his mission by saying that he came "not to be served but to serve others and to give his life as a ransom for many."[4] He came and willingly paid our spiritual death penalty in our place, on the cross, as a "ransom payment" for you and for me. (You may want to go back to complete the chart with the arrows pointing to the middle—by taking a pen and drawing a simple cross in the center of the diagram. That, ultimately, is what the twenty arrows point us to.)

So what are we supposed to do with all of this information? Two suggestions: (1) if you haven't done so already, study and reflect on it until you come to the point where you are able to grasp and acknowledge its truth—including the reality of your need for God's rescue and salvation; and (2) act on it by asking God to forgive your sins and to take control of your life. As basic as it may seem, it's this act of humble trust and repentance that God is patiently waiting for us to take.[5]

These two steps are so simple—and yet for some people they're so hard to do! Why is that? What are the barriers that can hold us back (or hold our friends back) from believing and doing what we now understand to be right? What are the impediments that can cause even committed believers to doubt? Here are ten common obstacles that can keep us, and the people we know, from experiencing a confident Christian faith.

BARRIER 1: LACK OF INFORMATION

You can't be truly confident about a faith you've adopted without really thinking about it—at least not in a way that will withstand the challenges that will inevitably come your way. And you can't will yourself into believing something you don't understand or agree with. So if what I've presented seems trustworthy, but you feel as if there are too many gaps in your understanding or too many questions still unanswered either to make the initial step of faith or to feel confident about a step you've already taken, then it's important that you slow down and do whatever it takes to find the necessary information. That might include going back over the twenty arrows and reflecting on the reasons presented there. But you might need to go deeper by studying some of the next-step books and resources I've listed in the endnotes and on pages 281 and 283.

Do whatever it takes to gain clarity, but let me caution you not to set the standard overly high for how much you need to know. Jesus said we need to come to him like children, with a simple, trusting faith.

Recently, my laser printer stopped printing. I opened its front panel and stared inside blankly, slowly realizing that I had no idea why it quit working. Then a deeper thought struck me: I also had no idea why it had ever actually *worked*, either. Likewise, I don't really understand how my computer functions, or even how the lightbulb in my desk lamp produces light and helps me see. I have a feeling I'm not the only one. We're surrounded by tools and technologies that we use every day, even though we don't fully grasp how they work.

Faith is much like that. We need to learn enough to make sure we're on the right path and embracing the right teachings, but we won't grasp the whole thing in depth—and we would be wise not to second-guess our decision until we do. It's like a courtroom situation: the jury takes in as much information as it can, but then it must reach a verdict based on that limited information, and within a limited time span.

And if you've never really accepted the Christian faith, one question to consider is this: How sure are you about your *current* faith? Remember, all the while that you're weighing the evidence and deciding about Christian beliefs, you're already operating out of some other belief system. In other words, you're not neutral. Right now you're living according to some set of ideas about spiritual realities and God (or lack of God). So let me ask you: Do you have better evidence for your current beliefs than you now have for Christianity? If not, it might be time to consider putting your trust in Christ.

BARRIER 2: LACK OF OPENNESS

This one is hard to admit—and often difficult to see in ourselves. For a variety of reasons, many people tend to approach new information while being limited by old presuppositions and prejudices. The liberal theologian Rudolf Bultmann stated famously in the early 1940s, "It is impossible to use electric light and the wireless and to avail ourselves of modern medical and surgical discoveries, and at the same time to believe in the New Testament world of spirits and miracles."[6] That kind of predetermined bias about what is possible or not possible will limit us or the people we know from authentically considering the actual evidence, especially when it points to the "world of spirits and miracles."

It's much better—and wiser—to simply be lovers of truth who open our minds and let the evidence lead us where it will. Along the way, we can figure out what really *might* be possible.

But lack of openness isn't a problem just for people who haven't accepted the Christian faith. Christians can be closed minded too—as many of our friends will be all too ready to attest. And this lack of openness isn't just a problem in relating to people with questions about your faith. It can sap your own confidence, as well. Think about it: Are there tough challenges to Christianity that you have deliberately chosen not to address? Is that because you're not sure your beliefs can stand up to that kind of scrutiny? As long as you're dodging the issues, you can never be completely confident that what you believe is the utter truth.

Now, there are some hard questions and some serious challenges related to the Christian faith, but in my experience, the deeper I look, the more confident I become. And the wealth of books, articles, and websites that offer credible information from highly credentialed teachers seems to increase by the day. One of those resources to be aware of is my recent book, *The Questions Christians Hope No One Will Ask (with answers)*, in which I respond to ten tough questions raised in a survey that we commissioned among one thousand Christians.[7]

Here's my advice: raise your doubts and questions, but then be willing to do some extra reading and research. If this faith is built on real facts as I've claimed, then it will stand the test of careful and honest scrutiny.

BARRIER 3: INTELLECTUAL DOUBT OR DISAGREEMENT

In response to my drawing of the twenty arrows on page 229, some people would offer a few "anti-arrows," or intellectual arguments that challenge and seemingly undermine the "preponderance of evidence" pointing to the middle of the chart. These would appear as arrows that point away from the center. The two most common objections like this that I've seen people raise are the problem of evil and the issue of suffering. Entire books have been written on these topics, but let me offer a few thoughts I think are relevant.

First, some people contend that the existence of evil means that there can't be a good, wise, and powerful God like the one I've described. That's because if he exists, he would surely want to put a stop to evil—and would have the power to do so. The fact that evil has not been stopped, the argument goes, indicates that this kind of a good, wise, and powerful God must not exist.

But the Bible teaches that the reason God has not yet stopped evil (which would involve putting a stop to the ones doing the evil—namely, *us* and *all of humanity*) is because of his patience toward us.[8] But there's an even more fundamental question that must be asked: *What is evil* in the absence of a Moral Lawgiver? Apart from the existence of a Moral Lawgiver (as we discussed in chapter 10), there can be no objective standard of right and wrong, or good and evil. So from an atheist's perspective, if you follow the reasoning all the way out, it all comes down to personal preferences or cultural norms. In other words, rape and murder may not be my cup of tea, but they could be yours. These things might be distasteful to me, but apart from a transcendent standard, I can't really insist that they're *wrong*.

But that presents a huge problem: you and I *really do know* that rape and murder are wrong. And this universal sense points us once again to a universal Standard Bearer who has woven a sense of morality into the very nature of what it means to be human.

So even the existence of evil points to the reality of a good God. And the arrow that seemed to be pointing away from the center is actually pointing back in, after all.

What about suffering? This one is difficult to address, especially in this limited space. But here are four thoughts:

First, no answer, no rationale, no philosophy, and no quote from the Bible will make you feel good about the difficult things you're going through in your life. Sometimes we make a mistake by trying to answer a question rather than just extending what is most needed at the time: love, mercy, comfort, and companionship. So if you're in pain or if you're suffering right now, I don't want to trivialize what you're enduring by offering what will inevitably feel like simplistic responses. Please feel free to skip down about seven paragraphs and come back to these thoughts about suffering at another time—and may God's comfort be with you in the interim.

Now, if you're still with me, it's worth pointing out that the kind of suffering we face in this life was predicted by Jesus. He warned us forthrightly that "here on earth you will have many trials and sorrows."[9] More broadly, Jesus and all the writers of the Bible describe a world where there is sin, conflict, betrayal, and war—much like what we see around us every day and hear about regularly on the nightly news.

So second, even though these hard things bring pain and loss, it's good to know that the faith system represented by Jesus is truthful in how he refuses to gloss over the harsh aspects of the world in which we live. Christianity doesn't try to convince us, as some religions do, that we're all basically good, sharing a common spark of divinity within our hearts and living in an increasingly utopian world where evil is a mere illusion. In sharp contrast to that misguided but popular worldview, Jesus cautioned us that there will be pain and suffering. The good news is that he immediately added these words of encouragement: "But take heart, because I have overcome the world."[10]

Third, Jesus didn't just warn us about suffering in this world; he personally experienced it in a measure greater than we can imagine. He cared for other people while lacking a home for himself. He faced resistance, ridicule, rejection, and scorn—and numerous attempts on his life—as he sought to teach and reach people just like you and me. And after three thankless years of doing this, he was finally betrayed by a friend, abandoned by his partners, falsely accused by the religious elite, tortured, and then killed in a brutal and shameful fashion between two common thieves. If anyone understands unjust suffering, and if anyone can offer us help and comfort in our times of need, it's Jesus, the Son of God, who endured such unthinkable things himself. He "understands our weaknesses, for he faced all of the same testings we do, yet he did not sin. So let us come boldly to the throne of our gracious God. There we will receive his mercy, and we will find grace to help us when we need it most."[11]

Finally, our experience of suffering points us logically back to God (in much the same way as the problem of evil). C. S. Lewis, in his earlier days as an atheist, used to ask, "If a good God made the world, why has it gone wrong?"[12] Here was the answer he later offered:

*My argument against God was that the universe seemed
so cruel and unjust. But how had I got this idea of
just and unjust? A man does not call a line crooked
unless he has some idea of a straight line. What was I
comparing this universe with when I called it unjust?
If the whole show was bad and senseless from A to Z, so
to speak, why did I, who was supposed to be part of the
show, find myself in such violent reaction against it? . . .*

*Thus in the very act of trying to prove that God did
not exist—in other words, that the whole of reality was
senseless—I found I was forced to assume that one part
of reality—namely my idea of justice—was full of sense.
Consequently, atheism turns out to be too simple. If the
whole universe has no meaning, we should never have
found out that it has no meaning: just as, if there were
no light in the universe and therefore no creatures with
eyes, we should never know it was dark. Dark would be
without meaning.*[13]

Aside from the issues of pain and suffering, another common
objection to Christianity is the apparent contradictions in
the Bible (such as differences among the Gospels of Matthew,
Mark, Luke, and John). For example, critics point to the fact
that one Gospel account says there was an angel at the tomb
on the first Easter morning, and another Gospel says there
were *two* angels. "How," they ask, "can you trust the New
Testament accounts about the Resurrection when the writers
can't even keep track of how many angels there supposedly
were at the empty tomb?"

First, most of these so-called contradictions are not serious problems. For example, if there were "two angels," then it's also accurate to say there was "an angel." Note that the second witness doesn't say "*only* one angel," which would have been a contradiction. If two reporters came and looked in my office right now, and if one of them later wrote, "Mark had a lamp on his desk," and the other mentioned in more detailed fashion that "Mark has two lamps on his desk," they would both be correct. A third observer might add even more facts, saying, "The guy must really like light—he has three lamps in his office." All three accounts would be accurate.[14]

Second, critics seem to overlook the fact that slight differences in eyewitness accounts of any event are actually earmarks of their truthfulness. It is when every witness says the exact same thing, in the exact same way, that we should become suspicious. The diversity in the Gospel descriptions tells us that the writers did not conspire to "get their stories straight" in order to foist a fable on us about something they made up.

When you've made it past Barrier 1: Lack of Information and Barrier 2: Lack of Openness, I think you'll find that addressing Barrier 3: Intellectual Doubt or Disagreement head-on will ultimately *increase* your confidence in the trustworthiness of the Christian faith.

BARRIER 4: LACK OF EXPERIENCE

Maybe you've noticed that most people today are no longer content with just information and ideas; we're after an *experience*. We don't just want coffee; we want a Starbucks experience. We don't just want a restaurant with good music;

we want to go to the Hard Rock Cafe. We don't just want a bookstore; we want a Barnes & Noble superstore, where we can have the coffee experience, listen to great music, sit in a nice leather chair, and peruse some good books—all in one place.

It's similar in the spiritual realm—most of us are no longer content with just finding facts and information, as important as those are; we want a genuine *spiritual experience*. I think that's appropriate. More than that, I believe it's a desire God puts in us, and that, if we seek him diligently and with a humble attitude, he will fulfill.[15] It reminds me of the verse in the Old Testament that says, "As the deer longs for streams of water, so I long for you, O God."[16] And there's another verse that gives a promise from God: "If you look for me wholeheartedly, you will find me."[17]

How can we do that? How can we look for the God we want to know and experience? The Bible is filled with clues. For example, we're told, "Humble yourselves before God. Resist the devil, and he will flee from you. Come close to God, and God will come close to you."[18] The Bible explains that "anyone who wants to come to him must believe that God exists and that he rewards those who sincerely seek him."[19] And Jesus encourages us to "keep on asking, and you will receive what you ask for. Keep on seeking, and you will find. Keep on knocking, and the door will be opened to you. For everyone who asks, receives. Everyone who seeks, finds. And to everyone who knocks, the door will be opened."[20]

There are a number of other practical ways to seek after God, in addition to taking to heart these kinds of promises in Scripture. One of the most basic is to get alone and quiet, and just talk to him. Tell him, in your own words, about your desire to know and experience him. Admit your sins and shortcomings, along with your worries and fears, and ask him to forgive you, to strengthen you, and to make his presence real to you. David, the psalm writer, tells us to "wait patiently for the LORD."[21] But know that waiting doesn't necessarily mean sitting still. Often I sense God the most when I go for a walk—especially out in nature—and quietly talk with him as I go.

Another way to experience God is in the presence of other Christians and people who are seeking God. This might be in a home Bible study or spiritual discussion group. Jesus said, "Where two or three gather together as my followers, I am there among them."[22] Often when you're talking about God with like-minded friends, or praying together with them, you'll sense that he is right there with you.

It's also important to know that worship services at churches can be great places to feel God's presence. This is true not only if you are a committed Christian, but also if you're still on a spiritual journey toward Christ. Maybe that's part of why the Bible says, "Let us not neglect our meeting together."[23] So seek out a church that is based on clear, biblical teaching, but one that also offers regular opportunities for extended, heartfelt worship. This can provide regular boosts to your relationship with God and help you develop a truly confident faith.[24]

BARRIER 5: LIFESTYLE ISSUES

This is another one of those personal issues that is easy to underestimate, but how you are living can have a huge impact on what you're open to embracing. If you perceive, for example, that genuinely following Jesus will require you to change certain aspects of your life that you'd rather not let go of, then you'll naturally find yourself looking for excuses to go in a different direction. It's like the story told about comedian W. C. Fields, who near the end of his life was seen reading the Bible, and when asked why replied, "I'm looking for loopholes, my friend. Looking for loopholes."

A more serious example is from the writings of Aldous Huxley, the well-known author and atheist who offered the following admission:

> I had motives for not wanting the world to have a
> meaning; consequently assumed that it had none,
> and was able without any difficulty to find satisfying
> reasons for this assumption. . . . For myself, as, no
> doubt, for most of my contemporaries, the philosophy
> of meaninglessness was essentially an instrument of
> liberation. The liberation we desired was simultaneously
> liberation from a certain political and economic system
> and liberation from a certain system of morality. We
> objected to the morality because it interfered with
> our sexual freedom.[25]

That was a vulnerable disclosure, but if we're honest, many people resist God because of what they know they'd have to change or give up, and many of us who claim to be committed Christians shy away from the full implications of that commitment because we want to hold onto some area of our lives that we know is wrong. Is that your situation? If it is, it will prevent you from fully embracing truth, and it will preclude you from gaining confidence in your faith.

So as you consider the implications of truly following Christ, try to pull back the covers on what is influencing your decision or perhaps putting a drag on it. What would you need to change or let go of? Often *that* is the issue much more than questions about the evidence for the miracles of Jesus or how many angels there were at his empty tomb.

Whatever the issue is, I'm confident that the surpassing benefits of knowing God and his forgiveness and leadership will far outweigh what you might need to alter or give up. As the apostle Paul so poignantly puts it, "I once thought these things were valuable, but now I consider them worthless because of what Christ has done. Yes, everything else is worthless when compared with the infinite value of knowing Christ Jesus my Lord. For his sake I have discarded everything else, counting it all as garbage, so that I could gain Christ."[26]

BARRIER 6: PERSONAL HURTS

Sometimes the below-the-surface impediment is not an intellectual question or a lifestyle issue, but a personal experience or wound that makes it hard to have confidence in Jesus Christ. Perhaps you were around someone who claimed to be a Christian but was a thoroughgoing hypocrite. Maybe you've said something like, "If that's what Jesus and his people are like, then I don't want to have anything to do with him or his church."

I've got news for you: that's *not* what Jesus is like. In fact, do you know who dislikes hypocrisy even more than you do?

Jesus![27] So he's right there with you in how you feel about many of the inconsistencies and shortcomings of people who claim to represent him.

If your personal hurts are of a different nature, all I can say is that God is your best source of healing and wholeness. I don't say that because I know your pain or experience, because obviously I don't—but God knows, and I'm fully convinced that he cares. He made you, and he loves you. Jesus is the one who said, "Come to me, all of you who are weary and carry heavy burdens, and I will give you rest. Take my yoke upon you. Let me teach you, because I am humble and gentle at heart, and you will find rest for your souls. For my yoke is easy to bear, and the burden I give you is light."[28]

Instead of resisting and running from God, move toward him, asking him for help and healing in the midst of your pain. He is the one who "understands our weaknesses, for he faced all of the same testings we do, yet he did not sin."[29] Therefore we are encouraged to "come boldly to the throne of our gracious God. There we will receive his mercy, and we will find grace to help us when we need it most."[30]

In addition, a solid, Bible-oriented church will often have people who can either offer counseling or refer you to recommended counselors in your area.[31] Professional help of this kind (from a Christian, if possible), can be an important link toward healing and health—and ultimately toward a more confident faith.

So don't let your wounds go untreated. They will just deepen and infect your spiritual life. The Bible warns us, "Watch out that no poisonous root of bitterness grows up to trouble you."[32] And Matthew assures us that God "will not crush the weakest reed or put out a flickering candle. Finally he will cause justice to be victorious."[33]

BARRIER 7: CONTROL ISSUES

Friedrich Nietzsche once declared boldly, "We deny God as God. . . . If the existence of this Christian God were *proved* to us, we should feel even less able to believe in him."[34] This is the same man who became known for his philosophy that life is all about "the will to power." He also made the infamous statement that "God is dead."[35]

Although Nietzsche took it to the extreme, his thoughts represent a struggle that many of us have: we desire to stay in control, relinquishing none of our freedom or autonomy to any outside forces or higher powers—God included.

C. S. Lewis describes the problem from a different angle, but in his characteristically insightful way:

> *There is one vice of which no man in the world is free; which every one in the world loathes when he sees it in someone else; and of which hardly any people . . . ever imagine that they are guilty themselves. . . .*
>
> *The essential vice, the utmost evil, is Pride. Unchastity, anger, greed, drunkenness, and all that, are mere fleabites in comparison: it was through Pride that the devil became the devil: Pride leads to every other vice: it is the complete anti-God state of mind. . . .*
>
> *In God you come up against something which is in every respect immeasurably superior to yourself. Unless you know God as that—and, therefore, know yourself as nothing in comparison—you do not know God at*

all. As long as you are proud you cannot know God.
A proud man is always looking down on things and
people: and, of course, as long as you are looking down,
you cannot see something that is above you.[36]

You might want to go back and read that passage again,
maybe a few times; it is penetratingly true, and yet its meaning is persistently elusive. Pride is, as Lewis describes, so easy
to see in others and yet so hard to detect in ourselves—and
it's completely devastating when left unchallenged. While all
of the other sins make you wonder whether God can accept
you, pride makes you foolishly wonder whether you'll accept
God—and his leadership for your life.

But spiritual confidence comes only when we approach
God on his terms. We've already looked at this advice:
"Humble yourselves before God."[37] And Jesus asked, "Why
do you keep calling me 'Lord, Lord!' when you don't do what
I say?"[38] We won't know God in a real way, and we won't
experience the full life he wants to give us, until we genuinely
make him our Lord, which means our Master or Leader.

In other words, we must allow *him* to be the one who is
in control.[39]

BARRIER 8: APATHY

This is one of the hardest obstacles to deal with because old-
fashioned apathy, by definition, doesn't care enough to get
too worked up about anything—including matters of faith.
In fact, we live in a secular society that seems to make a
studied effort to ignore or neglect true spirituality. Call it the
national religion of "whateverism."

And this is another impediment that doesn't just affect those outside the church. The attitude of apathy has seeped into our cultural water table, and it impacts people on every side of the spiritual equation and in every age group. Just ask some youth ministers what their biggest challenge is in working with church kids, and this issue will often be near or at the top of their list. Unfortunately, many pastors who minister to adults will report the same problem.

Maybe you can relate to this barrier on a personal level. You'd *like* to drill down to the core of your faith, to inspect the foundations of your belief system to make sure it's built on a solid foundation of facts and evidence. But you find it hard to muster the energy necessary, so instead you just settle with a halfhearted faith about which you feel neither confidence nor passion.

But here's some good news: the fact that you've read this far in a book about spiritual truth is a good sign that you have not yet succumbed to complete apathy. Let me urge you to take whatever level of interest you already have and expand on it. Fan it into a flame. Make your pursuit of spiritual confidence a front-burner issue.

Or, as Jesus challenged, do whatever it takes to seek after the "pearl of great value."[40]

BARRIER 9: FEAR

Sometimes spiritual hesitation and doubt go undefined—but they can stem from underlying fears that are very real. This can result, for example, from a natural discomfort with stepping into the unknown. Change is hard for almost everyone. It's always easier to stick with the status quo and put off new things for another day—a day that may never come. But it's better to face the discomfort now as you search for truth, confront your questions, or solidify your faith in Christ.

Your trepidation can also come from a sinister source. This may be a new thought to you, but according to Jesus and the clear teachings of the Bible, there is an ongoing but unseen spiritual battle raging in our hearts and minds. Jesus wasn't kidding when he said that Satan is like a thief who "comes only to steal and kill and destroy."[41]

This might seem easy to ignore or even write off completely, were it not for those inaudible, but very real, negative whisperings:

> *"Don't get too serious about these faith matters. You have far more pressing issues to worry about."*

> *"Today would not be a good day to renew your commitment. You can deal with that when you're a bit older."*

> *"You've got too much to do before letting go of your freedom and putting on a religious straightjacket."*

> *"You're really above all this. Everyone knows you're a good person—so what more could God ask of you?"*

> *"If you want to get right spiritually, you're going to have to try a lot harder. It's like the Bible says: 'God helps those who help themselves.'"*[42]

"You don't know enough yet. First you'll need to read the entire Bible—preferably in Greek and Hebrew. And you should probably enroll in seminary as well."

"You know too much—including how far you've fallen and how unworthy you are of a second chance. Seriously, God's getting sick of your pathetic pleadings."

I'm guessing that some of these conflicting and confusing messages are not new to you. As C. S. Lewis so colorfully illustrates in his book *The Screwtape Letters*, the devil is cunning, clever, and unrelenting in his efforts to sabotage our spiritual lives. But in our "enlightened" society, belief in the existence of an actual devil is out of fashion. The late Keith Green captured the mood of our culture when he sang a song that speaks from the perspective of Satan—"No One Believes in Me Anymore":

Oh, my job keeps getting easier
As time keeps slipping away
I can imitate your brightest light
And make your night look just like day
I put some truth in every lie
To tickle itching ears
You know I'm drawing people just like flies
'Cause they like what they hear
I'm gaining power by the hour
They're falling by the score
You know, it's getting very simple now
'Cause no one believes in me anymore.[43]

It's time we started believing—and fighting back. The apostle James tells us how in a passage we quoted part of earlier:

> *Humble yourselves before God.* Resist the devil, and he will flee from you. Come close to God, and God will come close to you. *Wash your hands, you sinners; purify your hearts, for your loyalty is divided between God and the world. Let there be tears for what you have done. Let there be sorrow and deep grief. Let there be sadness instead of laughter, and gloom instead of joy. Humble yourselves before the Lord, and he will lift you up in honor.*[44]

I'm glad to tell you that in the same conversation where Jesus warns us about the devil's plan to "steal and kill and destroy," he also says, "I am the gate. Those who come in through me will be saved. . . . My purpose is to give them a rich and satisfying life."[45]

A rich and satisfying life—one that flows out of a confident faith in Christ.

BARRIER 10: OVERSIMPLICITY

Okay, I'm not sure that "oversimplicity" is a real word, but I think it describes a real problem—one that is a normal human reaction to the unadorned message of God's gospel of grace. We find it hard to believe that the Good News can be as simple as the Bible says it is. We tell ourselves, *God can't just send Jesus to die on the cross and pay the penalty in my place. Trusting in Jesus might be a good thing to do, but it can't be enough. Somehow I've got to figure out a way to help earn it, to make myself better . . . to pay God back!*

By the way, this is a problem for many people who are just investigating and considering the message of Christ—but it's also an issue for many who have already put their trust in him. So much so that the apostle Paul had to warn the church in Galatia not to go back to their old ways of thinking by trying to add good works to the simple message of the gospel. Look at what Paul said to them: "How foolish can you be? After starting your Christian lives in the Spirit, why are you now trying to become perfect by your own human effort? Have you experienced so much for nothing? Surely it was not in vain, was it?"[46]

And so, down through the ages, countless religious systems have been devised—some quite elaborate—to try to provide ways for us to work our way back to God. Though he is unimaginably holy, we attempt to appease him and claw our way into his good favor. What's really confusing is that some of these payback schemes are promoted under the banner of Christianity. But they confound and confuse the uncomplicated message of God's grace, which is freely available to every one of us through faith in Jesus Christ.

Against this human tendency to make things more complicated than they are, I'll say it again: we need to *let Jesus speak for himself.* He's the one who straightforwardly summed it all up when he said these famous words:

> For God loved the world so much that he gave his one and only Son, so that everyone who believes in him will not perish but have eternal life. God sent his Son into the world not to judge the world, but to save the world through him. There is no judgment against anyone who believes in him.[47]

What does it mean to *believe* in Jesus? It includes accepting what he taught about himself: that he is God incarnate who came to earth to "seek and save those who are lost"—*namely, us*.[48] But more than just embracing a set of ideas ("right beliefs"), we need to receive the *person* who said he is the truth[49] ("take appropriate action"). Jesus wants to be not only our forgiver but also our leader and our friend. And it all starts when we call on him sincerely, by faith, for "everyone who calls on the name of the LORD will be saved."[50]

So let me urge you one more time: be a lover of truth. Seek it—and Jesus, who *is* Truth—with everything you've got, because he promised that if you'll seek, you will find. You'll find salvation, you'll find a new life of adventure, and you'll find out the benefits of living with a truly confident faith—in him.

CHAPTER FOURTEEN

FINDING A CONFIDENT FAITH

I'm woven in a fantasy, I can't believe the things I see
The path that I have chosen now has led me to a wall
And with each passing day I feel a little more like something dear was lost
It rises now before me, a dark and silent barrier between,
All I am, and all that I would ever want to be. . . .

KERRY LIVGREN, "THE WALL"[1]

My father's words were both freeing and frightening to me—at the same time.

I was freshly out of high school, living in my parents' home, working at a stereo store, and trying to figure out whether I should stay in that job, go to college, or do something else with my life. From a faith standpoint I was kind of a mess. I had been out on a prodigal excursion for several years—still believing the things I'd been taught growing up, but not living them out very well.

I loved my parents, but during that era I'd try to avoid getting caught in conversations that might become a bit too personal for my current comfort level. But therein lay the problem. In order to make it to the safety of my bedroom,

I had to get to a short staircase that led to the upper floor of the split-level house. This meant walking past the living room area near the fireplace where my dad would often sit at night reading the newspaper. There was no other way to get upstairs, except by climbing through a second-story window (which I had already tried a couple of times—it was not a good idea).

One particular evening I came home fairly late at night. I entered the house as quietly as possible, hoping to escape detection—and interrogation. But then, sure enough, I entered the living room and saw my father sitting by the fireplace. He seemed preoccupied as he gazed quietly into his newspaper, but I somehow felt that he was poised to ensnare me in a discussion I really didn't feel like having. So I tried to slip surreptitiously past the danger zone to the sanctuary of my room.

Unfortunately, because of my father's eagle eye and keen sense of timing, I got caught.

"*Mark*," my dad said in a gentle but abrupt voice that stopped me in my tracks. He looked up from the newspaper and asked, "Do you have a minute?"

"Sure . . ." I said, trying to sound as casual as possible. "What's up?"

"I've been wanting to talk to you about something," he replied. Sure that this couldn't be good, I asked him what it was about. "You're reaching the age, Son, when you're making important, life-changing decisions. And as your mom and I have been talking and praying about that, we've reached a conclusion I wanted to share with you."

Knowing he was probably not ramping up to tell me they

had decided to divvy up the inheritance funds early, I hesitantly replied, "Okay, what is it?"

"We wanted to tell you that we've done our best to raise you in the nurture and admonition of the Lord." (That's King James English from Ephesians 6:4. It means to teach your child how to follow and please God.) "We've done about all we can do to point you in the right direction in your faith, but you're already, what, eighteen years old?"

"Yep, almost nineteen," I replied.

"Well, you're a young man now, and you are at the age where you'll have to start deciding for yourself what you believe and how you're going to live your life. Our job as parents is pretty much finished. We can't make up your mind for you, and we don't want to try to force you to do or be anything you really don't want to."

Okay, I thought. *So far, so good.*

"So," he continued, saying those freeing but frightening words I alluded to earlier, "we want you to know that we're now giving you over to the Lord and putting you in his hands. We'll always be here to help and encourage in any way we can—and you know we want you to follow Jesus—but what you decide and do from here on out will ultimately be between you and God."

"Okay," I said, not quite sure how to react. "Thanks for letting me know." Then I turned and walked up the stairs to my room, feeling some relief that perhaps the pressure would finally be off to go to church on Sunday mornings, pretend to be religious, and so forth. But as I sat on the edge of my bed and weighed what he'd said, I realized the "giving you over to the Lord and putting you in his hands" part was a bit scary.

I mean, I could avoid—or trick—my *parents*, at least part of the time. But *God*? Wasn't he supposed to be everywhere, seeing everything we do and knowing every thought we think? That idea made me feel really uncomfortable.

Reflecting back now, years later, I can see that my parents were wise in how they handled me. They steered me toward truth my entire life, but when adulthood came, they let me chart my own course.

A few weeks after that pivotal discussion with my dad—when, at age nineteen, I got tired of playing religious games while living a hypocritical life—I finally made my move. It was not a momentous event—at least not on the surface; it was really more of a quiet affirmation of what I knew to be true and a decision to finally respond and act on that knowledge.

It was late in the evening. I was driving my car on the outskirts of our town. The prayer itself was simple. I don't remember whether I said the words out loud or just expressed them in my mind, but I guess it doesn't make any difference to God, who actually does know our thoughts. Basically, all I said was, *Dear God, I'm tired of pretending, going my own way, making a mess of my life, and wasting so much time. Please forgive my sins and take control of my life. Please accept me as your son, and I'll do my best to follow you from here on out—from now until eternity. In Jesus' name, amen.*

Brilliant bursts of fireworks? Nope. Miraculous signs, shooting stars, angels with special messages suddenly sitting in the backseat of the car? None of that. Just an awareness of God's presence and pleasure, a changed heart, a feeling of relief, and the sense that I was now beginning a truly revolutionized life.

That was the day that I found real *faith*—trust in the God who made and redeemed me, the God who would lead my life and begin to use me in at least a small way to help build his Kingdom.

At the time I would have said it was a confident faith. Thinking back to that early era in my walk with Christ, I think these verses from Romans 5 pretty well describe how I felt:

> *Since we have been made right in God's sight* by faith, *we have peace with God because of what Jesus Christ our Lord has done for us.* Because of our faith, *Christ has brought us into this place of undeserved privilege where we now stand, and we confidently and joyfully look forward to sharing God's glory.*[2]

Yes, during that early era I felt quite secure in what I believed. But it would be several years before I would experience a deep and genuine *confidence* in what I believed, and in many ways finding that kind of surety would be a lifelong journey—one I'm still traveling on today. And do you know what has helped develop that kind of confidence? The testing of my faith!

Look at the verses immediately following the ones I just quoted from Romans 5:

We can rejoice, too, when we run into problems and
trials, for we know that they help us develop endurance.
And endurance develops strength of character, and
character strengthens our confident hope of salvation.
And this hope will not lead to disappointment.[3]

For me, the tests were largely intellectual, including the objections to my beliefs that I endured in college (discussed in chapters 1 and 4). Also, my spiritual interactions with members of other world religions and Christian cults and sects—as well as those who were generally skeptical, including agnostics and a few full-blown atheists—all served to stretch and sharpen my faith in important ways. These were challenges I had to rise up to face through study, reflection, and prayer—but in the process this helped me develop, as the verse says, a measure of endurance, character, and finally real confidence.

Maybe you've been confronted with similar challenges. Or perhaps your "problems and trials" have come more through personal suffering and loss. These are things we would never wish or ask for, but that God sometimes allows into our lives. Yet if we'll lean into him for the help and wisdom we need to make it through them, they will serve to strengthen our trust in him. Truly it can become an example in our lives of the message in the well-known verse that comes a few chapters later:

*We know that God causes everything to work together
for the good of those who love God and are called
according to his purpose for them.*[4]

Looking back through the framework I've presented in this book, I came to Christ largely through the Traditional faith path—but included in what I'd learned growing up was at least enough rudimentary information to help me see that this was a reasonable faith built on a foundation of truth, not a blind or irrational belief system that would crumble under the weight of scrutiny.

And then, referencing our discussion in the last chapter concerning barriers to a confident faith, I had to overcome the fifth barrier, related to lifestyle issues that can hold us back from really following God, as well as some aspects of the eighth and ninth barriers: apathy and fear. I just thought I was having too much fun to let go and trust in Christ. I was afraid I'd lose the thrill of adventure in my life. Ironically, when I finally put my faith in him, the exact opposite happened; it's been an exciting journey of following and serving God, and it has included all kinds of amazing experiences that have taken me around the world.

Yes there are ups and downs, and candidly, every day is not necessarily "better than the day before." But God has opened doors to making a difference in the lives of others; to finding my purpose; to moving through life with an awareness that he is with me, that my life matters, and that I can make a real impact in the world; and to enjoying the assurance that I'm forgiven and don't have to live in fear, regret, or apprehension. On top of all of that, I know that someday I'm going to die—and then things will get even *better*.[5]

And finally, it has been the testing of my faith that has forced me to my knees to ask God for his help and guidance, as well as to my desk to research and study from the vast array of books, articles, and recorded messages that have provided a wealth of Evidential faith path–oriented data to bolster my beliefs. And I can honestly say, after thirty years of studying the information available to us from science, philosophy, history, archaeology, Scripture, and experience—in other words, the stuff of the Twenty Arrows of Truth we looked at in chapters 10 through 12—that I'm more convinced than ever that what we believe as Christians will withstand whatever objections people want to throw at it. That's because at bottom, it really is true!

This knowledge, based on seeing my beliefs overcome a variety of tests over the years, has helped me to find an increasingly *confident* faith—the kind of faith I'm convinced God wants you to experience as well.

And it's from that perspective, as one not just convinced of truth but also experiencing a rewarding relationship with the Creator, that I encourage you—no, *I strongly urge you*—to do whatever it takes for you to develop a confident faith yourself. Build on whatever strengths you've discovered from whichever faith path you've naturally been following, but then supplement it with the information and evidence that is so readily available through the sixth path, particularly the evidence from the Twenty Arrows of Truth presented in this book. Then review the barriers to a confident faith in chapter 13, and, over time and with God's help, overcome them. And finally, step into the exhilaration of experiencing a faith built upon facts, a solid faith in Christ, a faith that is real and that will withstand the test of scrutiny over the long haul.

It's so easy in the rush and busyness of life to view spiritual matters as otherworldly or optional—as the realm of saints and ascetics but not of ordinary, busy people like us. Yet there will come a day, and we're all approaching it faster than we think, when we'll be forced to face reality in the realm of spiritual truth.

With surprising candor, the late Steve Jobs of Apple Computer, a man not known for metaphysical musings, said this to Stanford's 2005 graduating class:

> *Remembering that I'll be dead soon is the most important tool I've ever encountered to help me make the big choices in life. Because almost everything—all external expectations, all pride, all fear of embarrassment or failure—these things just fall away in the face of death, leaving only what is truly important.*[6]

I couldn't agree more. I would add only this: When considering matters of faith, why wait until we're close to death, hoping that we'll have the chance to "make our peace" and patch things up at the very end—when it's too late to discover the adventure or to influence others with the truth that we've finally embraced?

It doesn't make sense to wait, which is why my challenge

to you—as well as to the friends and family members whom you influence—is to consider and act upon these things *now*, so you can enjoy the benefits of a confident faith in Christ throughout the rest of your life here on earth, as well as later, into the next life.

> *Faith is the confidence that what we hope for will actually happen; it gives us assurance about things we cannot see.*
>
> HEBREWS 11:1

> *We are confident of all this because of our great trust in God through Christ.*
>
> 2 CORINTHIANS 3:4

NOTES

CHAPTER 1. WHAT IS FAITH AND WHO HAS IT?

1. This is according to the Centers for Disease Control and Prevention. See article (last updated May 14, 2009) at: www.cdc.gov/Homeand RecreationalSafety/Dog-Bites/biteprevention.html.
2. As reported on Feb. 24, 2012, in the online version of *The Telegraph*, which can be viewed at www.telegraph.co.uk/news/religion/9102740/Richard -Dawkins-I-cant-be-sure-God-does-not-exist.html.
3. David Van Biema, "God vs. Science," *Time*, November 5, 2006.
4. 2 Timothy 3:16, KJV
5. Our discussion centers on a major area of philosophy, known as *epistemology*—the study of knowledge. Though this topic can become quite detailed and academic, it has very practical implications concerning what is true and how we can be confident in our beliefs.

CHAPTER 3. THE RELATIVISTIC FAITH PATH

1. Transcribed and excerpted from a video of this exchange between Bill O'Reilly and Richard Dawkins on the Fox News television program *The O'Reilly Factor* on April 23, 2007, posted at www.youtube.com /watch?v=5w8OhiLU7cU. Accessed October 23, 2012.
2. John 18:38
3. Ronald Harwood, screenwriter for *The Pianist* (in "Story of Survival" in the DVD's bonus materials, starting at 7:20), Limited Soundtrack Edition, 2003.
4. Zechariah 8:19 tells us to "love truth and peace."
5. *Oxford Companion to Philosophy*, s.v. "Socrates."

CHAPTER 4. THE TRADITIONAL FAITH PATH

1. Shirley Jackson, "The Lottery," *New Yorker*, June 28, 1948. Emphasis added.
2. Part of an interview with Dr. Paul Copan in Lee Strobel's *The Case for the Real Jesus* (Grand Rapids, MI: Zondervan, 2007), 249–250.
3. Mark 7:5-8. This passage is also paralleled in Matthew 15:1-9.
4. Isaiah 29:13
5. To read Lee Strobel's story of moving from atheism to faith, along with many of the discoveries that changed his mind, see his powerful book, *The Case for Christ* (Grand Rapids, MI: Zondervan, 1998).

CHAPTER 5. THE AUTHORITARIAN FAITH PATH

1. David Johnson and Jeff VanVonderen, *The Subtle Power of Spiritual Abuse: Recognizing and Escaping Spiritual Manipulation and False Spiritual Authority within the Church* (Minneapolis, MN: Bethany House, 2005).
2. Thomas S. Kuhn, *The Structure of Scientific Revolutions* (Chicago: University of Chicago Press, 1996).
3. John Mellencamp, "The Authority Song."
4. 1 Thessalonians 5:21-22
5. Matthew 7:15-17
6. John 8:46
7. Mark 9:23-24
8. 1 Timothy 4:16
9. John 3:12. Norman Geisler and Ron Brooks comment about this verse in their book *When Skeptics Ask* (Grand Rapids, MI: Baker, 1996): "Jesus expected His accuracy in factually testable matters to be proof that He was telling the truth about spiritual matters that cannot be tested" (148).
10. www.utlm.org/onlineresources/smithsonianletter.htm. Accessed October 26, 2012.
11. www.utlm.org/onlineresources/smithsonianletter2.htm. Accessed October 26, 2012.
12. See Bill McKeever, "DNA and the Book of Mormon Record," online at www.mrm.org/topics/book-mormon/dna-and-book-mormon-record. Accessed November 6, 2012.
13. Deuteronomy 18:21-22
14. Robert and Gretchen Passantino, *Answers to the Cultist at Your Door* (Eugene, OR: Harvest House, 1981), 50–53.
15. I'm not implying that leaders should have no privacy—just that the pattern of their lives should be transparent and open, and reflect godly values, beliefs, and character.
16. 1 Thessalonians 1:5; Philippians 4:9

17. More information is available about Nabeel Qureshi and his ministry, Creed 26, at www.creed26.com.

18. Nabeel Qureshi, "Crossing Over: An Intellectual and Spiritual Journey from Islam to Christianity," online at http://www.answering-islam.org /Authors/Qureshi/testimony.htm. Accessed November 6, 2012.

CHAPTER 6. THE INTUITIVE FAITH PATH

1. *Star Wars Episode IV: A New Hope*, directed by George Lucas (1977).

2. Psalm 139:14, NIV

3. Bill Moyers, "Of Myth and Men," *Time*, April 18, 1999.

4. Maharishi Mahesh Yogi, *The TM Technique: Life in Accord with Natural Law* (Kamchai Mear District, Prey Veng Province, Cambodia: Maharishi Vedic University, 1978), VHS.

5. L. T. Jeyachandran, "Tough Questions about Hinduism and Transcendental Meditation," in *Who Made God?* ed. Ravi Zacharias and Norman Geisler (Grand Rapids, MI: Zondervan, 2003), 163–164.

6. Napoleon Hill, *Think and Grow Rich* (San Diego: Aventine, 2004), 221. Originally published by the Ralston Foundation, Meriden, CT, 1937.

7. Ibid., 234, 236.

8. Rhonda Byrne, *The Secret* (New York: Atria, 2006), 56.

9. Malcolm Gladwell, *Blink: The Power of Thinking without Thinking* (New York: Little, Brown, 2005), 3.

10. Ibid., 4.

11. Ibid., 5.

12. Ibid., 5–6.

13. Ibid., 6.

14. Ibid., 7.

15. Ibid., 8.

16. 2 Corinthians 2:13

17. Blaise Pascal, *Pensées* (New York: Penguin, 1995), 127.

18. L. T. Jeyachandran, "Tough Questions," 164.

19. Gladwell, *Blink*, 14–15.

20. Proverbs 14:12

21. Jeremiah 17:9

22. John 10:27

CHAPTER 7. THE MYSTICAL FAITH PATH

1. This conversation took place during a dialogue between Mormons and Evangelical Christians at Mariners Church in Irvine, California, Spring 2007.

2. See Revelation chapter 11.

3. Robert L. Millet, *Getting at the Truth: Responding to Difficult Questions about LDS Beliefs* (Salt Lake City: Deseret, 2004), 36.

4. Ibid. Emphases added.

5. Ibid., 37. (Millet is quoting Ezra Taft Benson [president of the Church of Jesus Christ of Latter-Day Saints from 1985–1994] in *A Witness and a Warning: A Modern-Day Prophet Testifies of the Book of Mormon* [Salt Lake City: Deseret, 1988], 13, 31.) Emphasis added.

6. Ibid., 37–38. (Millet is quoting Gordon B. Hinckley [president of the Church of Jesus Christ of Latter-Day Saints since 1995] in *Faith, the Essence of True Religion* [Salt Lake City: Deseret, 1989], 10–11.) Emphasis added.

7. Ibid., 38. (Millet is quoting Boyd K. Packer, "Conference Report," October 1985, 104, 107.)

8. Ibid., 39. Emphasis added.

9. Ibid., 41.

10. See, for example, 3 Nephi, chapters 12–14, which are almost identical to the Sermon on the Mount in Matthew 5–7 of the King James Version of the Bible, including the additions in the KJV made for clarification and put in italics by the English translators. This is interesting in light of the fact that the original Book of Mormon purportedly was written more than a millennium before the King James Bible was produced in 1611.

11. These spiritual forces are referred to in passages such as 2 Corinthians 11:14 and Galatians 1:8-9.

12. 1 Thessalonians 5:21-22

13. 1 Thessalonians 5:19-20

14. For more information on Mormon teaching, see Bill McKeever and Eric Johnson, *Mormonism 101: Examining the Religion of the Latter-Day Saints* (Grand Rapids, MI: Baker, 2000).

15. For further reading on the topic of Islam and Jesus, see Norman Geisler and Abdul Saleeb, *Answering Islam* (Baker, 2002).

16. For details of Joseph Smith's contradictory accounts of his original vision, see Wesley Walters' "Joseph Smith's First Vision: Fact or Fiction?" (Mormonism Research Ministry), online at www.mrm.org/first-vision. Accessed November 6, 2012.

17. See McKeever and Johnson, *Mormonism 101* (Grand Rapids, MI: Baker, 2000), chapter 16, "Lamanites, The Seed of Cain, and Polygamy."

18. For many of the details on these "new revelations" and other issues, see Dr. Walter Martin, *The Maze of Mormonism* (Vision House, 1987).

19. A powerful book that details the internal struggles and inconsistencies within the Watchtower Bible and Tract Society (the Jehovah's Witness headquarters) is Raymond Franz, *Crisis of Conscience: The Struggle between Loyalty to God and Loyalty to One's Religion* (Commentary

Press, 2002). Franz was a former leader in the governing body of the Jehovah's Witnesses.

20. Acts 17:11

21. Galatians 1:8-9, NIV

22. I'm not denying the importance of praying and asking God for guidance as we assess truth claims and figure out what to believe. But this is not to be done in a vacuum, ignoring what we already know. And we should never pray and ask God whether something is true or okay if he has already made it clear that it is not.

23. Matthew 4:5-7

24. Bill McKeever, "As God Is, Man May Be?" (Mormonism Research Ministry) online www.mrm.org/lorenzo-snow-couplet. Accessed October 26, 2012.

25. Robert L. Millet, *Getting at the Truth: Responding to Difficult Questions about LDS Beliefs* (Salt Lake City: Deseret, 2004), 65. Note that the *Book of Moses and Doctrine and Covenants* (D&C) are part of the standard works of the Mormon faith.

26. Even this teaching is confusing, since Mormons often say that the one God who they worship is the Heavenly Father—but then they also claim to be the "Church of Jesus Christ." I've had the chance to question high level leaders of the Mormon church about this, and their answer seemed to imply that they worship both the Heavenly Father *and* Jesus Christ. But since they deny the biblical doctrine of the Trinity (that there is one God who eternally exists in three persons: Father, Son, and Holy Spirit), this equates to worshiping not one God, but two.

27. Isaiah 43:10, 12-13

28. Isaiah 45:21-22

29. Malachi 3:6

30. I realize that some Mormon teachers try to make the claim that they are not polytheistic because although they believe in many gods, they only worship one. But some Hindus similarly believe in many gods yet focus their worship on only one, such as Brahma, Vishnu, Shiva, or even Kali—but that narrower focus doesn't make them any less polytheistic.

31. Galatians 1:8, NIV. Emphasis added.

32. 2 Corinthians 11:14-15

33. 1 John 4:1, NIV

34. For one of many examples, see Deuteronomy 18:9-13.

35. Acts 9:1-9, 17-19

36. Augustine, *Confessions*, condensed version online at http://www.christianbooksummaries.com/archive.php?v=3&i=35. Accessed November 6, 2012.

37. Pascal never spoke of that night. The only way we know about it is that he had sewn the parchment with his account into his jacket, and it was

discovered after his death. This was later included in a compilation of his teachings, based on fragments of his writings, and called Pascal's *Pensées*.

38. 1 Thessalonians 5:21-22

CHAPTER 8. THE EVIDENTIAL FAITH PATH

1. These traditional Zen koans can be found online at terebess.hu/english /zen.html. Accessed November 6, 2012.

2. This "enlightening" explanation can be found online at http://thezenfrog .wordpress.com/2007/05/08/a-collection-of-zen-koans-and-stories-from-the-compilation-101-zen-stories. Scroll down to the end of "The Sound of One Hand." Accessed October 26, 2012.

3. Norman L. Geisler and Frank Turek, *I Don't Have Enough Faith to Be an Atheist* (Wheaton, IL: Crossway, 2004), 54–55.

4. William Lane Craig, *Reasonable Faith*, rev. ed. (Wheaton, IL: Crossway Books, 1994), 40.

5. Patrick Zukeran, "Archaeology and the Old Testament," (Probe Ministries). The text of this article can be found online at www.probe.org (use the site's search box). Accessed November 6, 2012.

6. Norman L. Geisler, *Baker Encyclopedia of Christian Apologetics* (Grand Rapids, MI: Baker, 1999), 702.

7. Richard Dawkins, *The Blind Watchmaker* (New York: Norton, 1986), 1. Emphasis added.

8. Ibid., 21. Emphasis added.

9. Ibid., 36. Emphasis added.

10. Ibid., 5.

11. Richard Dawkins, *The God Delusion* (New York: Houghton Mifflin, 2006), 158. Emphasis added.

12. Marilynne Robinson, "Hysterical Scientism: The Ecstasy of Richard Dawkins," *Harper's* (November 2006).

13. Antony Flew and Roy Abraham Varghese, *There Is a God: How the World's Most Notorious Atheist Changed His Mind* (New York: HarperCollins, 2007), xiv-xv.

14. Ibid., xvi–xviii.

15. Associated Press, "Famous Atheist Now Believes in God," December 9, 2004.

16. Lee Strobel, "Why Top Atheist Now Believes in a Creator," featured an interview between Lee Strobel and Dr. Antony Flew, and originally appeared in Strobel's online newsletter on November 2, 2006. It is now available at www.freerepublic.com/focus/f-news/1731763/posts. Dr. Flew made similar statements in an interview with Dr. Benjamin Wiker, which can be viewed at www.tothesource.org/10_30_2007/10_30_2007.htm. Accessed November 9, 2012.

CHAPTER 9. ASSESSING THE SIX FAITH PATHS

1. "The Logical Song," words and music by Rick Davies and Roger Hodgson. Copyright © 1979 Almo Music Corporation/Delicate Music/Universal Music Publishing Group. All rights reserved.
2. This conclusion is backed up in my understanding of the writings of numerous Christian philosophers and teachers, including John Warwick Montgomery, Norman Geisler, R. C. Sproul, E. J. Carnell, William Lane Craig, and my primary philosophical mentor, Stuart C. Hackett.
3. 1 Thessalonians 5:21
4. 1 John 4:1
5. Matthew 7:7
6. John 8:32
7. This quote is one Bob often told me and others, but it was put in print, along with his overall story, by Gretchen Passantino-Coburn, Bob's wife and ministry partner for many years. The full story can be found online at www.answers.org/news/article.php?story=20071004173254274. Accessed October 31, 2012.
8. I recently contributed to a book written in honor of Bob and Gretchen Passantino, along with a number of other authors and teachers whose lives were affected by them. The book was edited by Norman Geisler and Chad V. Meister and is called *Reasons for Faith: Making a Case for the Christian Faith* (Crossway, 2007).

CHAPTER 10. HOW SCIENCE AND LOGIC POINT TOWARD SPIRITUAL TRUTH

1. See Mark 9:23-25, where Jesus hears and honors this man's vulnerable request.
2. Michael Denton, *Evolution: A Theory in Crisis* (Bethesda, MD: Adler & Adler, 1986), 328, 342.
3. Psalm 19:1
4. Romans 1:20
5. Richard Dawkins, *The God Delusion* (New York: Houghton Mifflin, 2006), 158.
6. "Star Survey Reaches 70 Sextillion," CNN.com, July 23, 2003. Available online at www.cnn.com/2003/TECH/space/07/22/stars.survey. Accessed October 31, 2012.
7. Hugh Ross, *The Creator and the Cosmos* (Colorado Springs: NavPress, 1993), 111–114.
8. Lee Strobel, *The Case for a Creator* (Grand Rapids, MI: Zondervan, 2004) 130–131. The quote of Fred Hoyle is from "The Universe: Past and Present Reflections," Engineering & Science, November 1981.
9. Ibid., 133–134.
10. Patrick Glynn, *God: The Evidence* (Roseville, CA: Prima, 1999), 54–55.

11. Ibid., 53.

12. Francis S. Collins, *The Language of God: A Scientist Presents Evidence for Belief* (New York: Free Press, 2006), 1–2.

13. Ibid., 2.

14. Ibid., 1, 3.

15. Lee Strobel, *The Case for a Creator* (Grand Rapids, MI: Zondervan, 2004), 71.

16. From *Unlocking the Mystery of Life* (Murietta, CA: Illustra Media, 2002), DVD. See www.illustramedia.com.

17. For a comprehensive presentation of the arguments related to DNA, see Stephen C. Meyer, *Signature in the Cell: DNA and the Evidence for Intelligent Design* (New York: HarperOne, 2009).

18. There are several versions of the cosmological argument. This one is called the *kalam* version, which is presented and defended in detail by many contemporary thinkers, especially William Lane Craig in his scholarly book *The Kalam Cosmological Argument* (Eugene, OR: Wipf & Stock, 1979). Craig also discusses it with Lee Strobel in *The Case for a Creator*, and Chad Meister offers a straightforward explanation of it in his excellent book *Building Belief* (Grand Rapids, MI: Baker Books, 2006).

19. Albert Einstein, *Ideas and Opinions*, Modern Library Edition (New York: Random House, 1994), 43.

20. To use this point to try to argue that God must also have had a beginning is to misunderstand the meaning of *God*. He is eternal and did not have a beginning—and therefore does not have or need a cause. Unlike the universe and everything that is part of it, God is the cause behind the whole chain of effects and the only being sufficient to have produced such amazing effects, as we'll see.

21. Robert Jastrow, *God and the Astronomers*, 2nd ed. (New York: W.W. Norton, 1992), 103.

22. Ibid., 13.

23. Stephen Hawking and Roger Penrose, *The Nature of Space and Time* (Princeton, NJ: Princeton University Press, 1996), 20.

24. Stephen Hawking, in his more recent book (with Leonard Mlodinow), *The Grand Design* (New York: Bantam Books, 2010), says, "Because there is a law such as gravity, the universe can and will create itself from nothing. . . . Spontaneous creation is the reason there is something rather than nothing, why the universe exists, why we exist. It is not necessary to invoke God" (page 180). But this is a declaration of faith—not an explanation of science. It is, in effect, invoking the miracle without the miracle-worker. For a series of refutations of these claims, see William Lane Craig's responses (both written and recorded) at www.reasonablefaith.org/william-lane-craig-on -hawking-and-mlodinows-grand-design. Accessed November 6, 2012.

25. Genesis 1:1

26. Jastrow, *God and the Astronomers*, 107.
27. 1 Timothy 4:2, NIV
28. C. S. Lewis, *Mere Christianity* (New York: HarperOne, 2001), 6–7.
29. Romans 2:15
30. Lee Strobel, *The Case for Faith* (Grand Rapids, MI: Zondervan, 2002), 250–251.

CHAPTER 11. HOW EVIDENCE FOR THE BIBLE POINTS TOWARD SPIRITUAL TRUTH

1. Norman Geisler and William Nix, *A General Introduction to the Bible* (Chicago: Moody, 1986), 176–177. For a fuller list and discussion, see Michael Brown, *Answering Jewish Objections to Jesus, vol. 3: Messianic Prophecy Objections* (Grand Rapids, MI: Baker, 2003).
2. My two favorite versions are the New Living Translation (the NLT, which I'm mostly quoting in this book) and the New International Version (the NIV). Both are marked by a strong combination of accuracy to the original languages and clarity for ordinary people.
3. The biblical canon is the collection of authoritative writings comprising the Bible—the writings that passed the test and proved to have the credentials to be considered part of God's revelation.
4. *The Gnostic Bible*, ed. Willis Barnstone and Marvin Meyer (Boston: Shambhala, 2003), 46, 48, 69, as cited by Lee Strobel in *The Case for the Real Jesus* (Grand Rapids, MI: Zondervan, 2007), 27.
5. 1 John 1:1, NIV
6. Luke 1:1-4
7. John A. T. Robinson, *Redating the New Testament* (Eugene, OR: Wipf & Stock, 2000). Originally published in 1977 by Westminster Press, Philadelphia.
8. People do try to rewrite history, of course—there are some who deny the Jewish Holocaust and others who try to persuade us that President Kennedy and Elvis Presley are really still alive and living on an island somewhere—but their foolishness is evident to any serious observer.
9. For details on outside historical confirmation for Jesus and the early church, see Gary Habermas, *The Historical Jesus: Ancient Evidence for the Life of Christ* (Joplin, MO: College Press, 1996). See also Josh McDowell and Bill Wilson, *He Walked Among Us: Evidence for the Historical Jesus* (Nashville, TN: Thomas Nelson, 1993).
10. I once took a tour of a Hindu temple and was candidly told by the official Hindu tour guide, "Our religion is so old we don't even know where it comes from."
11. If you're concerned about the differences in the translations, visit a Christian bookstore and read the same passages from several different

versions (or view them online at a site such as www.biblegateway.com). You'll see that they use a variety of English words to get at the same meaning. The differences can actually help you better understand the original message, which is why publishers also produce "interlinear" versions, which put four, six, or sometimes even eight different translations in columns next to each other. One caution, however: The New World Translation, produced by the Watchtower Society of the Jehovah's Witnesses, is not a reliable translation, nor is it supported by reputable biblical scholars. It is contradicted at numerous key points by every reliable version, including the New Living Translation, the New International Version, the New American Standard Bible, the classic King James Version, and many others.

12. See Justin Taylor, "An Interview with Daniel B. Wallace on the New Testament Manuscripts," Mar. 21, 2012, The Gospel Coalition blog, which can be read at http://thegospelcoalition.org/blogs/justin taylor/2012/03/21/an-interview-with-daniel-b-wallace-on-the-new -testament-manuscripts/.

13. For a detailed discussion of the New Testament manuscripts, see chapter 3, "The Documentary Evidence," in Lee Strobel, *The Case for Christ* (Grand Rapids, MI: Zondervan, 1998).

14. Ibid., "An Interview with Daniel B. Wallace on the New Testament Manuscripts," Mar. 21, 2012.

15. John Ankerberg said this during the taping of his program, *The John Ankerberg Show*, with guest Lee Strobel, in the fall of 2007 (to be aired later). This was related to me by Lee Strobel.

16. Frederic G. Kenyon, *The Bible and Archaeology* (New York: Harper and Row, 1940), 288–289.

17. For more information see Norman Geisler and William Nix, *A General Introduction to the Bible* (Chicago: Moody Publishers, 1986).

18. For a great overview of the archaeological evidence, see chapter 5, "The Scientific Evidence: Does Archaeology Confirm or Contradict Jesus' Biographies?" in Lee Strobel, *The Case for Christ* (Zondervan, 2003). Also, for some of the newest findings in this area, see Craig Evans, *Jesus and His World: The Archaeological Evidence* (Louisville, KY: Westminster John Knox Press, 2012).

19. Sir William Ramsay, *The Bearing of Recent Discovery on the Trustworthiness of the New Testament* (London: Hodder and Stoughton, 1915), 222, as cited in Josh McDowell, *More Than a Carpenter* (Carol Stream, IL: Tyndale, 1977), 39. For an example of Ramsay's writings that are in print today, see *St. Paul the Traveler and Roman Citizen* (Grand Rapids, MI: Kregel Publications, 2001).

20. Nelson Glueck, *Rivers in the Desert: A History of the Negev* (New York: Farrar, Straus, and Cudahy, 1959).

21. William F. Albright, "Retrospect and Prospect in New Testament Archaeology," in *The Teacher's Yoke*, E. Jerry Vardaman, ed. (Waco, TX: Baylor University Press, 1964), 189, as cited in *When Skeptics Ask*, Norman Geisler and Ron Brooks, eds. (Grand Rapids, MI: Baker, 1996), 202.

22. Dr. Paul Vitz makes a great point when he describes how some people project their disappointment and frustration with their earthly fathers into the sky and deny the heavenly Father who actually is there. See Paul Vitz, *Faith of the Fatherless: The Psychology of Atheism* (Dallas: Spence, 2000).

23. Proverbs 27:6, KJV

24. See, for example, Luke 6:6-11 and Luke 13:10-17—especially verse 14, which reports that "the leader in charge of the synagogue was indignant that Jesus had healed her on the Sabbath day. 'There are six days of the week for working,' he said to the crowd. 'Come on those days to be healed, not on the Sabbath.'"

25. Isaiah 53:6

26. Lee Strobel, *The Case for Christ: The Film* (Lionsgate Home Entertainment, 2007).

27. Isaiah 53:5

28. Zechariah 12:10

29. Matthew 27:46, NIV

30. Psalm 22:1, 7-8, 14-18, NIV

31. For example, in Matthew 27

32. Micah 5:2

33. 2 Samuel 7:12-16

34. Isaiah 7:14

35. Isaiah 9:6

36. Isaiah 53:3

37. Zechariah 11:12

38. Isaiah 52:14

39. Isaiah 53:5-6

40. Isaiah 53:9

41. Psalm 16:10

42. This quote is from Louis Lapides, a Jewish man who was convinced by the evidence of prophecy many years ago to trust in Jesus as his Messiah. He is now the pastor of a church. His story, and this quote, can be found in Lee Strobel, *The Case for Christ* (Grand Rapids, MI: Zondervan, 1998), 183.

43. If you want to know the odds of *forty-eight* messianic prophecies being fulfilled by one person, see Lee Strobel, *The Case for Christ* (Grand Rapids, MI: Zondervan, 1998), 183.

44. Luke 24:25-26

45. Luke 24:32

CHAPTER 12. HOW HISTORY AND EXPERIENCE POINT TOWARD SPIRITUAL TRUTH

1. For instance, Jesus' enemies quibbled over whether his disciples had worked on the Sabbath day by eating grain as they walked through a field. Jesus answered their objection in Luke 6:3-5. He answered similar challenges related to his healing of a man's hand on the Sabbath in the verses that follow (Luke 6:6-11).

2. John 8:46

3. John 5:18

4. Abdullah Yusuf Ali, *The Holy Qur-an: Text, Translation, and Commentary* (Lahore, Pakistan: Shaikh Muhammad Ashraf, 1938), Surah 40:55. Emphasis added.

5. For clarity, in keeping with the way that days were counted in that culture, parts of three days would be referred to simply as "three days." Jesus was crucified on Good Friday, so he was dead and in the grave for the latter part of Friday, all day Saturday, and the very early part of Sunday, prior to his resurrection. In their way of counting, that was three days.

6. Matthew 28:13. See verses 11-15 for the story.

7. Gary Habermas and Michael Licona, *The Case for the Resurrection of Jesus* (Grand Rapids, MI: Kregel, 2004), 108–109.

8. John 20:28

9. 1 Corinthians 15:3-8

10. Acts 2:22-24, 32-33, 36

11. Acts 2:37-38

12. According to the statistics at www.adherents.com (accessed November 6, 2012), there are currently about 2.1 billion Christians, and 1.5 billion Muslims.

13. Acts 26:26

14. See Acts 6:8–8:1.

15. Acts 8:1; 9:1

16. The account of Saul's (Paul's) conversion is in Acts 9.

17. James is mentioned by name in the early creed that is recorded in 1 Corinthians 15.

18. See 1 Corinthians 15:7.

19. You can read about Paul's conversion in Acts 9.

20. Simon Greenleaf, *The Testimony of the Evangelists: The Gospels Examined by the Rules of Evidence* (Grand Rapids, MI: Kregel Classics, 1995), 8. Originally published in 1874.

21. Sir Lionel Luckhoo, "The Question Answered." This article can be found online at www.hawaiichristiansonline.com/sir_lionel.html. Select the link for "The Question Answered" booklet. The quote appears on the last page of the article. Accessed November 6, 2012.

22. Josh McDowell, *More Than a Carpenter* (Carol Stream, IL: Tyndale, 2004), and *Evidence That Demands a Verdict* (San Bernardino, CA: Here's Life, 1979). An updated edition of *Evidence That Demands a Verdict* was published by Authentic Lifestyle in 2004, and an updated edition of *More Than a Carpenter* has been released by Josh and his son, Sean, McDowell (Carol Stream, IL: Tyndale, 2009).

23. Viggo Olsen published his story in a booklet titled "The Agnostic Who Dared to Search," (Chicago: Moody Press, 1974). He also published stories of his time in Bangladesh, in *Daktar: Diplomat in Bangladesh* (Chicago: Moody Press, 1973), and *Daktar II* (Chicago: Moody Press, 1990). Also, his story is presented in summary form in Lee Strobel, *The Case for a Creator*.

24. John 14:6

25. John 8:32

26. Matthew 11:28-30

27. Greenleaf, *Testimony of the Evangelists*, 11.

CHAPTER 13. BREAKING THROUGH THE BARRIERS TO CONFIDENT FAITH

1. My calculations are based on statistics given at www.unitedjustice.com /death-statistics.html and at www.cougarinfo.org. Accessed August 6, 2012.

2. Richard Dawkins, during a lecture at the 1992 Edinburgh International Science Festival, as cited by Alister McGrath, in *Dawkins' God: Genes, Memes, and the Meaning of Life* (Malden, MA: Blackwell, 2004), 84.

3. Luke 6:46

4. Matthew 20:28

5. I go into more depth on the meaning and logic of the gospel in my small book, *The Reason Why Faith Makes Sense* (Carol Stream, IL: Tyndale House Publishers, 2011). I wrote this to reinforce the faith of Christians, and also to be an inexpensive gift they can give to non-Christian friends, to help them understand and embrace faith in Christ.

6. Rudolf Bultmann, *New Testament and Mythology and Other Basic Writings* (Minneapolis, MN: Fortress, 1984).

7. Mark Mittelberg, *The Questions Christians Hope No One Will Ask (with answers)* (Carol Stream, IL: Tyndale House Publishers, 2010). Specifically, we had the Barna organization call 1,000 Christians all over the country and ask them what faith questions they would feel most uncomfortable being asked by a friend or colleague. We then compiled a list of the top ten questions, and those formed the list of challenges I address in the book.

8. See 2 Peter 3:9-10, which says, "The Lord isn't really being slow about his promise, as some people think. No, he is being patient for your sake. He does not want anyone to be destroyed, but wants everyone to repent. But the day of the Lord will come as unexpectedly as a thief." Also see verse 15 in that same chapter.

9. John 16:33 (the first half)

10. John 16:33 (the second half)

11. Hebrews 4:15-16

12. C. S. Lewis, *Mere Christianity* (New York: Macmillan, 1960), 45.

13. Ibid., 45–46. Emphasis his.

14. For answers to 800 of these kinds of challenges and issues related to the Bible, I recommend Norman Geisler and Thomas Howe, *When Skeptics Ask: A Popular Handbook on Bible Difficulties* (Victor, 1992). Also see Gleason L. Archer, Jr., *New International Encyclopedia of Bible Difficulties* (Zondervan, 2001).

15. For clarity, I'm not talking in this section primarily about spiritual experiences that tell you who God is (as we discussed earlier regarding the Mystical faith path)—though I believe God will sometimes provide those. I'm referring here to encounters with the living God that *confirm* what logic and evidence have told you (through the Evidential faith path, as well as, perhaps, information you've gained through other faith paths), but which take you beyond intellectual information into actual personal experience.

16. Psalm 42:1

17. Jeremiah 29:13

18. James 4:7-8

19. Hebrews 11:6

20. Matthew 7:7-8

21. Psalm 27:14

22. Matthew 18:20

23. Hebrews 10:25

24. To find a great list of generally relevant and accessible churches, visit www.willowcreek.com and click on "Find a Church." If you hit "Map It," you can search by city, state, or zip code.

    To find the kinds of discussion groups I mentioned check with a national ministry called Q Place at www.QPlace.com. They have quality leaders hosting spiritual discussion groups all over the USA and in a number of other countries as well.

    Also, there is a similar ministry that has groups meeting around the world, called Alpha. Check them out at www.AlphaNA.org (Alpha North America).

    Finally, if you're interested in starting a group yourself, I highly recommend reading Garry Poole's helpful book, *Seeker Small Groups: Engaging Spiritual Seekers in Life-Changing Discussions* (Zondervan, 2003).

25. Aldous Huxley, *Ends and Means* (London: Chatto & Windus, 1969), 270, 273. Emphasis added.

26. Philippians 3:7-8

27. See, for example, Luke 6:41-42 and all of Matthew 23.

28. Matthew 11:28-30

29. Hebrews 4:15

30. Hebrews 4:16

31. Again, a good place to start your search is at www.willowcreek.com under "Find a Church."

32. Hebrews 12:15

33. Matthew 12:20 (Matthew is quoting from the Old Testament book of Isaiah.)

34. Friedrich Nietzsche, *The Antichrist*, trans. Anthony Ludovici (Amherst, NY: Prometheus, 2000), 72. Originally published in 1895.

35. Have you seen the T-shirts? On one side they say, "'God is dead,' signed Nietzsche." On the other side it says, "'Nietzsche is dead,' signed God."

36. Lewis, *Mere Christianity*, 108–109, 111.

37. James 4:7

38. Luke 6:46

39. As difficult as yielding control of your life to God might seem, keep in mind that he is the one who created all things, who made us, who knows our thoughts before we even think them, and who loves us with an everlasting love. When you begin to grasp who he really is, putting him in the driver's seat is not such a scary proposition!

40. Matthew 13:46 says, "When he discovered a pearl of great value, he sold everything he owned and bought it!"

41. John 10:10, NIV

42. The Bible does not say this. Rather, it teaches that God helps those who give up on helping themselves—and instead reach out to the Savior. Ephesians 2:8-9 tells us that "God saved you by his grace when you believed. And you can't take credit for this; it is a gift from God. Salvation is not a reward for the good things we have done, so none of us can boast about it."

43. "No One Believes in Me Anymore," words and music by Keith Green and Melody Green. Copyright © 1978 April Music. All rights reserved.

44. James 4:7-10. Emphasis added.

45. John 10:9-10

46. Galatians 3:3-4

47. John 3:16-18

48. Luke 19:10

49. From Jesus' words, describing himself, in John 14:6

50. Romans 10:13

CHAPTER 14. FINDING A CONFIDENT FAITH

1. "The Wall," by Kerry Livgren. Copyright © 1976 Don Kirshner Music (BMI). Used by permission. All rights reserved.

2. Romans 5:1-2. Emphasis added.

3. Romans 5:3-5. Emphasis added.

4. Romans 8:28

5. Philippians 1:21 says, "For to me, living means living for Christ, and dying is even better."

6. Steve Jobs, speaking for the 2005 commencement at Stanford University, June 12, 2005. The transcript can be found online at http://news-service. stanford.edu/news/2005/june15/jobs-061505.html. Accessed November 6, 2012.

FOR FURTHER READING

The Questions Christians Hope No One Will Ask (with answers),
   Mark Mittelberg (Tyndale, 2010)
The Reason Why: Faith Makes Sense, Mark Mittelberg (Tyndale, 2011)
The Case for Grace, Lee Strobel (Zondervan, 2013)
The Case for Christ, Lee Strobel (Zondervan, 1998)
The Case for Faith, Lee Strobel (Zondervan, 2000)
The Case for a Creator, Lee Strobel (Zondervan, 2004)
The Case for the Real Jesus, Lee Strobel (Zondervan, 2007)
The Case for the Resurrection of Jesus, Gary R. Habermas and
   Michael R. Licona (Kregel, 2004)
More Than a Carpenter, Josh and Sean McDowell (Tyndale, 2009)
Know Why You Believe, Paul Little (InterVarsity, 1970)
Mere Christianity, C. S. Lewis (Macmillan, 1952)
The Purpose Driven Life, Rick Warren (Zondervan, 2002)
Jesus Among Other Gods, Ravi Zacharias (W, 2000)
Putting Jesus in His Place, Robert Bowman and J. Ed Komoszewski
   (Kregel, 2007)
Mormonism 101, Bill McKeever and Eric Johnson (Baker, 2000)
On Guard: Defending Your Faith with Reason and Precision,
   William Lane Craig (David C. Cook, 2010)
Reasonable Faith, William Lane Craig (Crossway, 2008)
Building Belief, Chad V. Meister (Baker, 2006)
I Don't Have Enough Faith to Be an Atheist, Norman Geisler and
   Frank Turek (Crossway, 2004)
Cold-Case Christianity, J. Warner Wallace (David C. Cook, 2013)

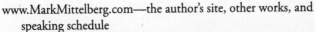

FOR ONLINE RESEARCH

www.MarkMittelberg.com—the author's site, other works, and speaking schedule

www.LeeStrobel.com—features video clips on a variety of faith questions and issues

www.ReasonableFaith.org—site of William Lane Craig, a leading theologian and philosopher of religion

www.Apologetics315.com—one of the premier sites on Christian apologetics

www.Creed26.com—site of Nabeel Qureshi, whose story is told in chapter 5

www.RisenJesus.com—site of Michael Licona, author and expert on the resurrection of Christ

www.JesusCentral.com—information about Jesus from primary sources

www.JesusFactOrFiction.com—site related to a DVD apologetics tool which features the author and others

www.WillowCreek.com—click "Find a Church" for relevant places to explore and grow in faith

www.QPlace.com—link for finding a spiritual discussion group in the United States and a growing number of other countries

www.AlphaNA.org—link for finding an Alpha group in North America

ACKNOWLEDGMENTS

I would never have been able to complete this book without first having been the recipient of the support, encouragement, and prayers of the following people:

Lee Strobel, my close friend and ministry partner, who spurred me on and helped me move forward from the inception to the completion of this project. He said it well when he once wrote, "We're each other's biggest boosters. I have more confidence in Mark than he has in himself, and that's how he feels about me. That makes for a terrific combination!" It was my turn to be on the receiving end of that encouragement, and I am deeply grateful.

To Heidi, my incredibly supportive and patient wife, and our two great (and now grown) children, Emma Jean and Matthew—thanks for the prayers and cheers, not to mention coffee and snacks at odd times of the day and night, and occasional trips to the park for Frisbees and a chase with our little pal, Charlie (the Cavalier). And, as always, thanks for the prayers and support from our parents, Hillis and Jean Hugelen, and Orland and Ginny Mittelberg.

Thanks to Dr. Chad Meister for your philosophical wisdom and editorial input. Your generous sharing of knowledge and insights served me and the readers of this book immeasurably. Thanks, too, to Brad Mitchell, for your faithful encouragement and prayers. To Tom Chapin and Nabeel Qureshi, thanks for your important feedback at critical points.

I'm also indebted to my philosophical mentors, both near and far: the late Bob Passantino and his wife, Gretchen, William Lane Craig, Norman Geisler, and especially the late Stuart Hackett—including the early influence of a dusty old textbook Dr. Hackett assigned to his students: *The Ways of Knowing* by William Montague.

A special thanks to Jon Farrar, Ron Beers, Jane Vogel, and the entire team at Tyndale House Publishers. And appreciation to Don Pape, my first literary agent, who helped get the process started, and to Lee Hough at Alive Communications, for keeping me on track.

To all of you—and to any I failed to mention—my heartfelt thanks.

ABOUT THE AUTHOR

MARK MITTELBERG is a bestselling author, a sought-after speaker, and a leading outreach strategist. He is the primary author (with Lee Strobel and Bill Hybels) of the celebrated *Becoming a Contagious Christian* training course, which has been translated into more than twenty languages and used to train 1.5 million people to talk naturally about their relationship with Christ.

Mark's newest book, *Confident Faith: Building a Firm Foundation for Your Beliefs*, was written to encourage believers as well as spiritual seekers to explore what they believe and why, so they will end up with a faith they're really sure of. A previous book, *The Reason Why: Faith Makes Sense*, is an update of a classic that has touched millions of lives over the past century—recreated by Mark to help a new generation understand the significance of Jesus' death on the cross. He also wrote *The Questions Christians Hope No One Will Ask (with answers)*, which deals with the ten issues believers most want to avoid—but must not. Prior to that, Mark collaborated with Lee Strobel to develop *The Unexpected Adventure*, a story-driven devotional designed to encourage Christians in sharing their faith.

Mark's other books include *Becoming a Contagious Church*, which sets forth an innovative blueprint for church-based evangelism, and the classic bestselling book, *Becoming a Contagious Christian*, which he coauthored with Bill Hybels. In addition, Mark was a contributing editor for *The Journey: A Bible for the Spiritually Curious*; a contributor to *Reasons for Faith: Making a Case for the Christian Faith*, edited by Norman Geisler and Chad Meister; and a contributor to *God Is Great, God Is Good: Why Believing in God Is Reasonable and Responsible*, edited by William Lane Craig and Chad Meister—and winner of the 2010 *Christianity Today* award for best book on apologetics.

Mark was the evangelism director at Willow Creek Community Church in Chicago for seven years and for the Willow Creek Association for a decade. He was an editorial consultant and periodic guest for Lee Strobel's *Faith under Fire* television show. He and Strobel have been ministry partners for twenty-five years, and they now codirect The Institute at Cherry Hills, in Highlands Ranch, Colorado (TheInstituteAtCherryHills.org).

After receiving an undergraduate degree in business, Mark earned a master's degree in philosophy of religion, graduating magna cum laude from Trinity Evangelical Divinity School in Deerfield, Illinois. He also received an honorary doctor of divinity degree from Southern Evangelical Seminary in Charlotte, North Carolina. Mark and his wife, Heidi, have two grown children and live near Denver.

You can visit Mark's website at MarkMittelberg.com and follow him on Twitter at @markmittelberg.

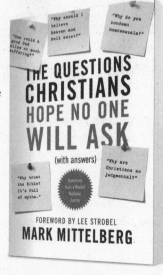

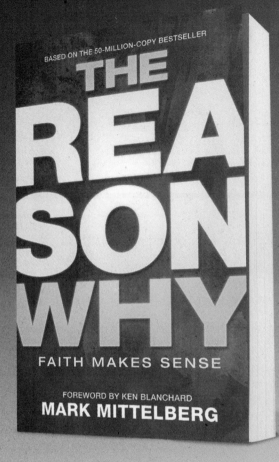

Online Discussion *guide*

TAKE *your* TYNDALE READING EXPERIENCE *to the* NEXT LEVEL

A FREE discussion guide for this book is available at bookclubhub.net, perfect for sparking conversations in your book group or for digging deeper into the text on your own.

www.bookclubhub.net

You'll also find free discussion guides for other Tyndale books, e-newsletters, e-mail devotionals, virtual book tours, and more!